Lights and Shadows in Confederate Prisons

CHAPTER I

The First, or Forenoon, Battle of Winchester, Indecisive—Sheridan's and Early's Mistakes—The Capture.

"WAR IS HELL," said our great strategist, General W. T. Sherman. According to its latest code, with few or no exceptions, the end justifies the means, and, if necessary to success, it is right to do wrong.

Fifty years ago one of the fairest regions on earth was that portion of Virginia extending southwesterly about a hundred and twenty miles from Harper's Ferry to the divide beyond Staunton, where rise the headwaters of the James. Walled in by the Blue Ridge on the southeast and parallel ranges of the Alleghanies on the northwest, it takes its name from the beautiful river which winds along its length, and which the Indians poetically christened Shenandoah (Daughter of the Stars!). When some three hundred of us prisoners of war walked wearily a hundred miles from Winchester to Staunton in September, 1864, it was still rich and lovely. A few weeks later, the necessities of war made it a scene of utter desolation.

> Grant had rightly concluded [says Sheridan[1]], that it was time to bring the war home to a people engaged in raising crops from a prolific soil to feed the country's enemies, and devoting to the Confederacy its best youth. I endorsed the program in all its parts; for the stores of meat and grain that the valley provided, and the men it furnished for Lee's depleted regiments, were the strongest auxiliaries he possessed.

Accordingly Grant issued orders with increasing emphasis, particularly in August and September, to make the whole region "a barren waste," to

> destroy or carry off the crops and animals; do all possible damage to railroads; seize stock of every description; take away all negro laborers so as to prevent further planting; hold as prisoners of war, if sympathizing with the rebellion,

> all male citizens under fifty years of age capable of bearing arms, etc.

In obedience to these commands, Sheridan engaged with alacrity in the work of destruction. In a few weeks he reported as follows:

> I have destroyed 2000 barns filled with wheat, hay, and farming implements; over 70 mills filled with flour and wheat; and driven in front of my army 4000 head of stock.

Said one of his officers who knew whereof he was speaking, "A crow flying through the valley would have to carry his own rations, for he could pick up nothing!"

At Winchester, the principal town in the Shenandoah Valley, one hundred and fifty miles N. N. W. of Richmond, with a population of about four thousand, the 19th of that September was a day of glory but also of sorrow. Four thousand six hundred and eighty of the Union Army, killed and wounded, told how dearly Sheridan's first great victory was gained.

The battle was fought over three, four, or five square miles, east and north from Winchester, for the most part near the Opequon Creek, from which it is sometimes called the "Battle of the Opequon." To reach the field, the bulk of Sheridan's army, starting at three o'clock in the morning from Berryville ten miles east, had to pass through a gorge in which for a considerable distance the turnpike extends towards Winchester. Sheridan's plan at first was to bring his army, except Merritt's and Averell's Divisions of Torbert's Cavalry, through the defile, post the Sixth Corps on the left, the Nineteenth on the right, throw Crook's Army of West Virginia across the Staunton turnpike (leading southwest from Winchester), and so cut off all retreat up the valley. Meanwhile those two cavalry divisions were to make a long detour on our right to the north from Berryville, and close in upon the Confederate left. Sheridan felt sure of victory, for we outnumbered the enemy nearly two to one. Had our army got into position early in the morning, we should have captured or destroyed the whole of them.

At early dawn McIntosh's Brigade of Wilson's Division of Torbert's Cavalry dashed through the ravine, closely followed by Chapman's Brigade and five batteries of horse artillery. Sheridan and his staff followed. They surprised and captured a small earthwork, and, though fiercely assaulted, held it till the van of the Sixth Corps relieved them.

The narrow pass of the Berryville pike was so obstructed by artillery, ambulances, ammunition wagons, etc., that it was nearly eight o'clock before the Sixth Corps, which should have been in position with Wilson's Cavalry at sunrise, began to arrive; and it was fully two hours later when the Nineteenth Corps debouched and deployed. Here was miscalculation or bad management or both.

This long delay, which the quick-moving cavalry leader Sheridan had not foreseen nor provided for, gave time for Early to call in the strong divisions of Generals Gordon, Breckenridge, and Rodes, from the vicinity of Stephenson's Depot several miles away. They left Patton's Brigade of Infantry, and a part of Fitzhugh Lee's Cavalry to oppose Torbert.

Hearing nothing from Torbert, who had now been gone seven or eight hours on his circuitous route, Sheridan suddenly changed his whole plan of action, a perilous maneuver in the face of an active enemy while the battle is already raging intermittently. Instead of flinging Crook's Army of West Virginia, 17 regiments and 3 batteries, across the Staunton pike, to front northeasterly and cut off all possible retreat of the Confederates, he determined to move it to our right and deploy it in line with the Nineteenth. Doubtless this was best under the circumstances, though it left to the enemy the broad smooth highway as a line of retreat up the valley.

Grover's Division (2d of the Nineteenth Corps) in four brigades formed line of battle in front and to the right of the gorge. In touch on the left was Ricketts' Division of the Sixth Corps, and resting on Ricketts' left was Getty's Division of the same corps. Getty had 16 regiments in line; Ricketts, 12 with 6 batteries; Grover, 20 with 3 batteries.

Had Sheridan been able to strike Early by half-past eight with the Sixth and Nineteenth, he would have crushed him in detail. Had Early massed the divisions of Gordon, Breckenridge, and Rodes, and hurled them at the mouth of the canyon at ten o'clock while half of the Nineteenth was still entangled in it, he would probably have split our army into three parts, and destroyed those already arrived.

It was now eleven o'clock, and the Army of West Virginia at last emerged from the defile. To make room for its movement in our rear behind Grover's Division, and to hold the enemy in play until it should have taken its place on the right of the Nineteenth, and perhaps to await there the appearance of Torbert's Cavalry, it was desirable that Grover should advance. Sheridan of course meant the whole front of the Sixth and Nineteenth to keep in a continuous line. At first it seemed to me that the regiments of the Nineteenth overlapped; but the lines of advance were slightly divergent, and wide breaks began to appear between battalions. Especially on the left of the Nineteenth a large and widening gap appeared; for Ricketts had been instructed to guide on the Berryville pike, and that bore away to the left and south.

My battalion, the veteran Thirteenth Conn. Infantry, should have been led by my Colonel, C. D. Blinn: but he was sick the night before, and in the morning, at the crossing of the Opequon, he fell out, and left the command to me. He had no part in the battle. Our Thirteenth deserves a passing notice. It was the favorite regiment of General Birge, its first colonel.[2] When he was made brigadier, the regiment entered the brigade commanded by Colonel E. L. Molineux. Birge was never so happy as when riding into action, and Molineux, who had been severely wounded in the same battle with me, was not over-cautious. My regiment and both brigades, the first and second of Grover's Division, had caught the spirit of those two commanders. Quite generally they mistook the forward movement for an immediate charge.

We had been under an intermittent fire for some time, but now the advance intensified the conflict. The chief anxiety of good soldiers at such a time, as I often noticed, is to get at the enemy as soon as possible, and cease to be mere targets. Their enthusiasm now accelerated their pace to a double-quick, and was carrying them too far to the front. Birge and Molineux endeavored in vain to check their rapidity. My battalion, I think, was nearest the rebel line.

Between eleven and twelve the divisions of Getty, Ricketts, and Grover, forty-eight regiments in all, to which were attached eight light batteries with reserve artillery, began to move forward. It was a grand spectacle. At first the movement was steady, and we thought of Scott's lines,

The host moves like a deep-sea wave,
Where rise no rocks its pride to brave,
High-swelling, dark, and slow.

But all is quickly changed.

Looking back upon that scene after the lapse of more than fifty years, its magnificence has not yet faded. I see as in a dream our long bending wave of blue rolling slowly at first but with increasing speed, foam-tipped with flags here and there and steel-crested with Birge's bayonets yonder; glimpses of cavalry in the distance moving as if on wings with the lightness of innumerable twinkling feet; numberless jets of smoke across the fields marking the first line of Confederate infantry, their musketry rattling precisely like exploding bunches of firecrackers; batteries galloping to position, the thunder of a dozen smiting the ear more rapidly than one could count; the buzz, hiss, whistle, shriek, crash, hurricane of projectiles; the big shot from batteries in front and from Braxton's artillery on our right ripping up the ground and bounding away to the rear and the left; horses and riders disappearing in the smoke of exploding shells; the constant shouting of our officers indistinctly heard, and now and then the peculiar well-known "rebel yell"; and finally the command, HALT! LIE DOWN! Molineux and Birge were too far to the front, and the line must be rectified. Ricketts, as we pressed forward, had thrown Keifer's Brigade (2d of Third Division, Sixth Corps), seven regiments, into the broadening interval directly in front of the mouth of the gorge; but it was not sufficient.

It was now Early's opportunity; but he was hours too late, just as Sheridan had been. He had seen our Sixth Corps and Nineteenth emerge and deploy, had beheld our rapid and somewhat disorderly approach, had noted the widening spaces between our battalions and divisions, had observed the havoc wrought by his artillery and musketry, ten thousand of our soldiers seeming to sink under it; had had time to mass his forces; and now it was "up to him" to hurl them against our centre. It was the strategy inaugurated by Epaminondas at Leuctra and perfected by Napoleon in many a hard battle, breaking the enemy's centre by an irresistible charge, dividing and conquering. Rodes had been killed at a battery in front of our brigade. His veterans and Gordon's, six thousand strong[3] constituted the charging column. Neither Sheridan nor any other Federal historian appears to have done justice to this charge. Pickett's at Gettysburg was not more brilliant.

With yells distinctly heard above the roar they advanced. The batteries on each side redoubled their discharges. From our irregular line of infantry extending more than a mile blazed incessant sheets and spurts of flame, the smoke at times hiding the combatants. Gordon was heading toward the now nearly empty ravine. My horse had just been shot under me. I lost two in that fight. Dismounted I walked from the right of my battalion to the left, cautioning my men against wasting their ammunition, bidding them take sure aim, pick out the rebel officers, and not fire too high. They were shooting from a recumbent position, or resting on one knee; lying flat on their backs to reload. As I reached the left, I glanced to the right and saw several of them starting to their feet, and a little further on, two or three began to run back. I rushed to the spot shouting, "Back to your places!" I saw the cause: the regiments on our right were retreating. I was astounded, for we were expecting an order to advance instantly. At that moment Lieutenant Handy, an aide of our brigade commander, rode up, pale, excited, his hands flung up as if in despair. My men were springing to their feet.

"What are those orders?" I demanded.

"Retreat, retreat! get to the rear as fast as possible," he replied.

"Battalion, rise up; shoulder arms—" I commanded. Before I could finish the order, one of Sheridan's staff came on a swift gallop, his horse white with foam.

"For God's sake, what does this mean?" said he; "this retreat must be stopped!"

"Battalion, lie down," I shouted; "our brigade commander ordered retreat!"

"It's all wrong. If this position's lost, all's lost. Here you have some cover. Hold it to the last. I'll bring supports immediately." Striking spurs into his steed, he vanished in the direction of the retreating regiments.

Except the few who had heard my command and remained in position, perhaps seventy-five or a hundred, who kept blazing away at the Confederates, rising a little to kneel and fire, Grover's Division, and all we could see of that of Ricketts, had gone to pieces, swept away like chaff before a whirlwind. Not a Union flag now in sight, but plenty of the "Stars and Bars!" Our sputtering fire checked some directly in front; but most of the on-rushing masses were deflected by the nature of the ground.

Out of our view and about half a mile in our rear was Dwight's Division, the First of the Nineteenth Corps. It had been left in reserve. It was in line of battle and ready for the onset. The confused fragments of Grover were rallied behind it. Had the ground been favorable, and had no unexpected opposition been encountered, Gordon would have crushed Dwight.

But in fewer minutes than we have occupied in describing this charge, a tremendous and prolonged roar and rattle told us that the battle was on behind us more than in front. Amid the din arose a quick succession of deafening crashes, and shot and shell came singing and howling over us from the left. Russell's Division (First of the Sixth Corps) comprising eleven infantry regiments and one of heavy artillery, behind which the broken battalions of Ricketts had been reassembling, was now smiting the right flank of Gordon's six thousand. Although the charge came too late we cannot but admire the strategy that directed it, and the bravery of the infantry of Gordon, Rodes, and Ramseur, as well as that of the cavalry of Lomax, Jackson, and Johnson, and of Fitzhugh Lee who fell severely wounded. But they had not foreseen the terrible cross-fire from Russell, who died at the head of his division, a bullet piercing his breast and a piece of shell tearing through his heart. Nor had they calculated on confronting the long line of Dwight, nine regiments with the Fifth New York Battery, all of which stood like a stone breakwater. Against it Gordon's masses, broken by the irregularities of the ground, dashed in vain. Under the ceaseless fire of iron and lead the refluent waves came pouring back. Our army was saved.

But we few, who, in obedience to explicit orders from headquarters, had held our position stiffly farthest to the front when all the rest of Grover's and Ricketts' thousands had retreated—we were lost. A column behind a rebel flag was advancing straight upon us unchecked by our vigorous fire.

Seeing that they meant business, I commanded, "Fix Bayonets!" At that instant the gray surges converged upon us right and left and especially in our rear. We seemed in the middle of the rebel army. In the crater of such a volcano, fine-spun theories, poetic resolves to die rather than be captured—these are point-lace in a furnace. A Union officer, Capt. W. Frank Tiemann of the 159th N. Y., Molineux's Brigade, was showing fight, and half a dozen Confederates with clubbed muskets were rushing upon him. I leaped to the spot, sword in hand, and shouted with all the semblance I could assume of fierce authority,

"Down with those muskets! Stop! I command you." They lowered them.

"Who the hell are you?" they asked.

"I'll let you know." Turning instantly to four or five Confederate officers, I demanded: "Do you mean to massacre my men?"

Two or three replied: "No. By G—! You've shown yourselves brave, and you shall be respected. Yes, you fought d—d well, seein' you had the d—dest brigade to fight against in the whole Confederate Army."

"What brigade are you?" I asked.

"Ramseur's old brigade; and there's nothin' this side o' hell can lick it."

"You're brave enough," said another; "but damn you, you've killed our best general."

"Who's that?" I asked.

"Rodes; killed right in front of you."

"I thought Early was your best General."

"Not by a d— sight. Old Jubal's drunk—drunk as a fool."

I was never more highly complimented than at this moment; but the stunning consciousness of being a prisoner, the bitterest experience of my life, the unspeakable disappointment, the intense mortification—these are even to this day poorly mitigated, much less compensated, by the excessive praises heaped upon me by those Confederate officers for my supposed bravery. That they were sincere I cannot doubt; for it was customary on the battle-field for the rebels to strip prisoners of all valuables, but no one of the fifty or one hundred near me was robbed. Tiemann, whose life I had perhaps saved, was even privileged to keep his canteen of whiskey, of which he gave me a drink by and by to keep me in good spirits! I realized the truth of Burns's lines:

Inspiring bold *John Barleycorn*!
What dangers thou canst make us scorn!
Wi' tippenny, we fear nae evil;
Wi' usquebaugh, we'll face the devil!

FOOTNOTES:

[1] *Personal Memoirs*, vol. i., p. 487.

[2] In New Orleans it was known as "Butler's Dandy Regiment"; for it was then better dressed than any other. It wore dark blue, which Birge had procured through his uncle, Buckingham, the war governor of Connecticut. At the siege of Port Hudson it had distinguished itself above all other regiments by furnishing as volunteers nearly one-fourth of the celebrated "Storming Column" of one thousand men called for by General N. P. Banks the second day after the disastrous assault on that fortress (June 14, 1863). Birge was selected by Banks to lead the forlorn hope.

[3] Six thousand is Gordon's statement in his *Reminiscences*, page 320.

CHAPTER II

At Winchester—On the Road thence to Tom's Brook, New Market, and Staunton.

THERE were two battles that Monday between Sheridan and Early, the first indecisive, though bloody, a drawn game; the second, after a comparative lull of several hours, a fierce struggle in which the whole front of the Sixth, Nineteenth, and Crook's Corps simultaneously advanced, and Torbert's Cavalry, arriving at last after their unaccountable delay upon our extreme right, made a magnificent charge crumpling up all the enemy's left. The victory was real, but not so complete as it should have been. Sheridan ought to have captured or destroyed the whole of Early's army. Instead, he had left them an open line of retreat. He took only five pieces of artillery, nine battle-flags, and some twelve or fifteen hundred prisoners; and, to use his own words, "sent the Confederates whirling up the valley."

In the recoil of Gordon's brilliant charge of six thousand about noon, we prisoners were swept along into Winchester, and then locked in the old Masonic Hall. The sociable guards took pains to emphasize the statement that George Washington, "glorious rebel" they called him, had presided as Grand Master in that very room!

After several hours we heard a great noise in the streets. Looking out we saw men, women, children, moving rapidly hither and thither, the current for the most part setting toward the southwest. The din increased; the panic became general; the Union Army was advancing on Winchester!

We were hustled into the street now filled with retreating hundreds, and were marched rapidly along the turnpike toward the setting sun. The road crowded with artillery, army wagons, common carriages, all pouring along in the stampede; a formidable provost guard enclosing us prisoners in a sort of hollow column; cavalry in front, flank, and rear; the fields on either side swarming with infantry, the whole of Early's army in retreat, we apparently in the middle of it; Sheridan's guns still booming in our rear—such was the scene as we two or three hundred prisoners were driven on. Our mingled emotions can be better imagined than described. The bitter regret that we had not been slain; the consciousness that we had done our whole duty in facing unflinchingly the storm of shot and shell, never retreating an inch; the evident respect and even courtesy with which I was personally treated; the inspiring certainty that our army was victorious, the unspeakable mortification of being ourselves prisoners of war!—we sorely needed all our philosophy and all our religion to sustain us.

Marching moodily along I was aroused from a sort of reverie by an experience far too common in those days. I had been sick the night before, and had worn my overcoat into battle. My horse was shot. The blood was spurting from him. As he seemed likely to fall, I leaped down. We were in the midst of a rapid advance and I had not time to throw off my overcoat. I was now carrying it swung over my arm. It was growing dark. A mounted soldier, whom I took to be an officer, rode up to my side and seized hold of the coat. He said, "I want that overcoat." I replied, "You can't have it." "I must have it." "You shan't have it." He tugged and I tugged, and as I was on foot and sober I nearly dragged him from his horse before he let go. During the tussle I repeatedly shouted, "Captain of the Guard—Help! Help!" The provost captain instantly came riding to the spot. "What's the matter?" he asked. "That rascal has tried to rob me of my overcoat," I answered, pointing to the villain who was beginning to slink away. The captain appeared to recognize him, said not a word to him, but whispered to me a moment later, "You are entitled to keep your overcoat."

We had had little breakfast and no dinner nor supper, but we suffered more from thirst than hunger. Can we ever forget it? Will the long flight never end? On through Kerrstown without halting we march, with promise of rest and water at Newtown; no rest nor water there. On from Newtown with assurance of water at Middletown. Five minutes at Middletown, and a little muddy water that seems to aggravate our thirst. Farther on we cross a bridge under which the water is dashing as if in mockery, and the cry "Water! water!" rises from a hundred lips, the guard joining, for they are suffering like ourselves. Some comfort in that! Past midnight we reach Strasburg and are halted around an old wooden pump. It is broken! No water there. Still on and on at a snail-pace, up and over the almost interminable stretch of Fisher's Hill. At three o'clock in the morning we arrive at a place known by the classical name of Tom's Brook about twenty-five miles from Winchester. Never was nectar more delicious than the water of this stream, nor downy pillow more welcome than the sod on its banks. Without blankets or covering we sank in each other's arms for mutual warmth on the dew-drenched grass; and blistered feet and aching limbs and hunger and thirst and suffocating despair are all forgotten!

Morning came unnoticed, except by those whom the keen cold permitted to sleep no longer. Towards noon we rose, washed without soap or towel, were made to form line, had our names taken, and received as rations a pint of flour per man, with a little salt, nothing else. How to cook or prepare the flour? We learned of the rebel guards a process not laid down in the cook-books. Mixing with water they made a stiff paste or dough. This they put around the end of a stick about the size and half the length of a walking cane. The end thus thickly coated they hold over a little fire till the smoke and flame have sufficiently hardened it. Then pull out your stick and you have a thick chunk or cylinder of bread, not quite so tough as a gun-barrel, but substantial!

I contrived to keep a little memorandum book. In it I noted down that there were three hundred and eleven of us prisoners; two lieutenant-colonels, two majors, four captains, nine lieutenants, and two hundred and ninety-four enlisted men. These were in the march from Winchester. A few may have been added to our number at Tom's Brook.

I have stated how it happened that none of those near me were robbed when captured. Those at a distance were not so fortunate; for, if circumstances permitted, the Confederates, being themselves sadly in want, often improved the opportunity to grab every article of value. At Tom's Brook I noted in my diary the following:

> Major A. W. Wakefield, 49th Pa. Cav., was robbed of hat, blanket, and $100 in money. Adjt. J. A. Clark, 17th Pa. Cav., was robbed of cap, boots, mug, pocket-book and money. Lieut. Harrison, 2d Regular Cav., was robbed of gold watch and money. Capt. John R. Rouzer, 6th Md. Inf., was robbed by an officer of hat and $20 in money. Lieut. Wesley C. Howe, 2d Mass. Cav., who recently died at Kansas City, Mo., was robbed by Lieut. Housel of the 6th Va. Cav., of

> silver watch, spurs, gloves, and $10 in money. Major August Haurand, 4th N. Y. Cav., was robbed of a watch and $60 in money.

It was a common practice to snatch from a Union prisoner his cap, and clap on in lieu of it a worn-out slouched hat; pull off his boots, and substitute a pair of clumsy old shoes. The plundering was so thoroughly done that it was poetically termed "going through" a captive!

As I was the senior officer among the prisoners, and we seemed likely to remain a long time there, I went to the Confederate commander and besought him to allow our three hundred prisoners to occupy a barn near by. He refused. I then asked that we be allowed to build wigwams for shelter, as there was abundant material at hand. This too was not permitted. I also begged in vain that a surgeon should be got to dress the wounds of some of the prisoners.

The second morning after our arrival, the sleeping men were aroused by the loud voice of Lieutenant Sargent of the 14th New Hampshire Regiment exclaiming: "If you give me any more of your lip, I'll annihilate you! I've but one arm" (his right arm was disabled by a shot), "but even with one arm I'll annihilate you on the spot, if you give me any more of your lip!" This was exceedingly gratifying, for it proved that at least two of us were not yet "annihilated!"

During our sojourn at Tom's Brook the Confederates labored hard to induce us to exchange our greenbacks for their paper currency. Our own was sadly depreciated, one dollar of silver or gold being equal to two of greenbacks; but one in United States paper was equal in purchasing power to eight of theirs. They argued that our money would certainly be forcibly taken from us by rapacious guards farther south, and kindly offered us four for one. Sergeant Reed of the Provost Guard was quite a character. Like Gratiano in *The Merchant of Venice*, he talked loud and long, speaking "an infinite deal of nothing." He had a mania for watches. He told me he now had twenty-seven which he had obtained from Yankee prisoners, always paying them in good Confederate money. He set his heart upon a little silver watch of mine, which he said he wished to buy and present to one of his lady admirers. I asked:

"Why do they admire you?"

"Because of my bravery," he replied; "none but the brave deserve the fair."

"If you are so brave, why are you back here? Why are you not at the front?"

"Colonel, I've been in the forefront of the hottest battles. I've been fearfully wounded. I'll be hanged if I haven't been one of the bravest of the brave. Twice, Colonel, I was shot all into inch pieces; and so now I'm put on light duty!"

On Thursday, the third day after our arrival, two "india-rubber men," circus performers, of the 22d Indiana Regiment, gave an exhibition of "ground and lofty tumbling" for the entertainment of their fellow prisoners. They had somehow contrived to retain the gaudy costume of the ring. They were really skillful. While we were watching with interest the acrobatic performance, a squadron of the Confederate General Imboden's Cavalry dashed past us. Sergeant Reed, who had just made me an offer for my watch, sprang to his feet, exclaiming: "I swear! there must be a battle going on in front, for there goes Jimboden's Cavalry to the rear! Sure sign! I'll be hanged if we ain't gettin' licked again!" We had heard the cannonading in the distance, but paid little attention to it. The Richmond papers, announcing that Fisher's Hill was impregnable to the whole Yankee army, were said to have been received about an hour before the heights were actually carried by storm. Again Early's army was not captured, but sent "whirling up the valley."

We prisoners thoroughly enjoyed the changed aspect of affairs. At first they marched us directly back a short distance up the slope towards the advancing Yankees; but they seemed suddenly to discover their mistake; they halted, faced about, and marched down. Hilarious and saucy, our boys struck up the song and three hundred voices swelled the chorus:

Rally round the flag, boys, rally once again,
Shouting the battle-cry of Freedom—
    The Union forever! hurrah, boys, hurrah!
    Down with the traitor! up with the star! etc.

till Captain Haslett of the provost guard came riding into the midst with savage oaths shouting, "*Silence!* SILENCE! SILENCE!"

Twenty-seven miles, first through stifling dust and then through pelting rain, past Hawkinstown, Woodstock, Edenburg, Mount Jackson, brought us to New Market. On the march Colonel Brinton of a Pennsylvania regiment, a new arrival, planned with me an escape. He had campaigned through the valley, was familiar with the lay of the land, and said he had friends among the inhabitants. Our plan was to run past the guards in the darkness. As a preliminary step I cut off my shoulder-straps which were very bright. Within half an hour Sergeant Reed came up to me and asked, "Colonel, where's your shoulder-straps?" I replied, "I don't wear shoulder-straps now I'm a prisoner." "But, Colonel," he answered, "I've been lookin' at them shoulder-straps since we left Tom's Brook. I wanted to buy 'em of you for a present to one of my girls. I'll be hanged if I don't believe you're goin' to try to escape, and so you've cut off your bright shoulder-straps. But, Colonel, it's impossible. I'll be hanged if I hadn't rather lose any six of the others than to lose you." The fellow stuck closer to me than a brother all the rest of that night; so close that he lost sight of Colonel Brinton, who actually escaped about midnight at a place called Edenburg! Almost immediately Sergeant Reed came to me and asked, "Colonel, where's that other Colonel?" I answered: "You ought to know; *I* don't!"—"I'll be hanged," said he, "if I haven't lost him, a-watchin' you!"

At New Market they put us into a dilapidated church building. "The wicked flea, when no man pursueth but the righteous, is bold as a lion," was repeatedly misquoted from the *Book of Proverbs*, and not without reason. We concluded if that interpretation was correct, we had reason enough for obeying the injunction in *Ecclesiastes*, "Be not righteous overmuch"; for the little jumpers were fearless and countless. They were reinforced by a Confederate deacon, who recommended two things: Confederate paper and "gospel piety"; the one would carry us safely through this world; the other through the next. He would be only too happy to furnish us the currency in exchange for our greenbacks. "Confederate treasury bills and true religion" was the burden of his song, till one of our literary officers, it was said, squelched him: "Deacon, your recipe of happiness, rebel paper and godliness—Confederate money and a Christian spirit!—reminds me of what Byron says in one of his wicked poems:

'Beyond all doubt there's nought the spirit cheers
Like rum and true religion!'"

He subsided.

We left New Market at noon, Saturday, September 24th, and marched all the afternoon and all night, past Harrisonburg, Mount Crawford, Mount Sidney, and Willow Springs, reaching Staunton, Va., about nine in the morning. On the march, forty-three miles in twenty-one hours, we were hungry; for the morning ration at New Market was scanty, and they gave us nothing more, except a small loaf of wheat bread. Some of the guard were kind to us. One of them, private John Crew, Co. E, 11th Alabama Regiment, unsolicited by us, and, so far as I am aware, without hope of any reward, would endeavor to bring us apples or other food, whenever we halted. I was careful to write his name in my diary.

As we trudged along, a lively discussion of slavery ensued. Lieutenant Howard of the provost guard was a learned champion of the "peculiar institution," and I was a pronounced abolitionist. He was an ardent "fire-eater," to use the term then in vogue, and I, who had lost my position as principal of the Worcester High School by my defense of John Brown, was equally intense. Both were pretty well "posted" on the subject. He seemed to be familiar with the Bible and the proslavery arguments, including drunken Noah's "Cursed Canaan!" Moses Stuart's *Conscience and the Constitution*, Nehemiah Adams's *Southside View of Slavery*, and Rev. Dr. —— (the name is gone from me) of Baltimore's Sermons. I was fresh from reading the arguments of George B. Cheever, Horace Bushnell, Henry Ward Beecher, Garrison, Phillips, and the rest. He proved that slavery among the Hebrews was a divine institution. I answered they were commanded to "undo the heavy burdens, let the oppressed go free, and break every yoke." He said Paul sent back the fugitive slave Onesimus to his master Philemon; I rejoined, "Paul said, 'I send him back, not as a servant, but above a servant, a brother beloved; receive him as myself.'" He quoted the Constitution of the United States, the article commanding that fugitive slaves should be delivered back to their masters; in reply I quoted from Deuteronomy the "Higher Law," "Thou shalt *not* deliver unto his master the servant which is escaped from his master unto thee." He quoted from the great speech of the magnificent Webster in the Senate, March 7, 1850, in which he urged all good citizens to obey the Fugitive Slave Law "with alacrity." Waxing hot, I quoted from Beecher:

> As to those provisions which concern aid to fugitive slaves, may God do so to us, yea and more also, if we do not spurn them as we would any other mandate of Satan! If in God's providence fugitives ask bread or shelter, raiment or conveyance at my hands, my own children shall lack bread ere they; my own flesh shall sting with cold ere they shall lack raiment. And whatsoever defense I would put forth for mine own children, that shall these poor, despised, persecuted creatures have at my hands and on the road. The man that would do otherwise, that would obey this law to the peril of his soul and the loss of his manhood, were he brother, son, or father, shall never pollute my hand with grasp of hideous friendship, nor cast his swarthy shadow athwart my threshold!

The lieutenant finally cited the examples of "those glorious southern patriots who led the rebellion against England during the first American Confederacy," Washington, Patrick Henry, Madison, Jefferson, "every one a slaveholder," he proudly exclaimed. I happened to be cognizant of their views, and responded with some vehemence: "But Washington's hands were tied so that he could not free slaves till his death. He said it was among his first wishes to see some plan adopted for putting an end to slavery. Patrick Henry declared, 'I will not, I cannot justify it.' Madison expressed strongly his unwillingness to admit in the national Constitution 'the idea that can hold property in man.'" In a rather loud voice I quoted Jefferson, who, in view of our inconsistency in violating the "self-evident truth" that "all men are created equal," solemnly affirmed, "*I tremble for my country, when I remember that God is just, and that his justice cannot sleep forever*!" I had some reputation as an elocutionist in those days, and Sergeant Reed, who was listening with open mouth, broke in with, "I'll be hanged, Colonel, if you warn't cut out for a preacher! By— I should like to hear you preach." The best reply I could make was: "You'll undoubtedly be hanged sometime; and if I were a minister, nothing would give me more satisfaction than to be present at your execution and preach your funeral sermon." He replied:

"Now, Colonel, you don't mean that. You don't think I'll ever be hanged!"—"Indeed I do, if you don't stop your profanity and general cussedness."—"I'll be hanged, if I will," was his last word to me.

CHAPTER III

At Staunton—Thence to Waynesboro, Meacham's, and Richmond.

AT Staunton we got a little more light on the value of Confederate paper. A chivalrous surgeon who accompanied the provost guard (Fontleroy, I think, was his name[4]) politely invited Captain Dickerman of the 26th Massachusetts and myself to take breakfast with him in a restaurant. We needed no urging. The Provost Marshal gave consent. The saloon was kept by a negro named Jackson. His entire stock of provisions consisted of nine eggs, the toughest kind of neck beef, bread and salt, coffee very weak, butter very strong. As we sat waiting, the doctor remarked with a lordly air that under ordinary circumstances he would not deign to eat with Yankees. I answered good-naturedly: "I'm as much ashamed as you can be; and if *you'll* never tell of it, *I* won't!" The food, notwithstanding its toughness, rapidly disappeared. Near the last mouthful the doctor said: "You two will have to pay for this breakfast, for I've no money." I had fifteen Confederate dollars remaining of twenty which I had received for a five-dollar greenback at Tom's Brook, and I answered: "Give yourself no anxiety; I'll foot the bill."—"Well, Jackson," said I to the sable proprietor, "what's the damage?" He replied, "I shan't charge you-ones full price. Let's see! Beef, seven; eggs, two—nine; coffee, three—twelve; bread and butter, three—fifteen; three of you—forty-five. I'll call it only thirty-six dollars!" I paid my fifteen; Captain Dickerman pleaded poverty; and the dignified doctor, who had so cordially invited us to partake of his hospitality, promised the disappointed Jackson that he would pay the balance at some future day ("the futurest kind of a day," was added in an undertone).

Rejoining the three or four hundred prisoners, we found, besides the Confederate guards, a great crowd of spectators swarming around us. One of them, a fine-looking young man, wearing the blue uniform of a United States captain, made his way through the group, and handed me a twenty-dollar Confederate bill! The following dialogue ensued:

"Here, Colonel, take that."

"I thank you much. Who are you, so kind to a stranger and an enemy?"

"I'm one whom you Yanks would hang, if you could catch me."

"Why so? Who are you?"

"I'm one of Morgan's guerrillas; wouldn't you hang me?"

"I think I should, if you had much of this stuff about you" (holding up the twenty-dollar bill); "I've just paid fifteen Confederate dollars for an imaginary breakfast."

"Good for you, Colonel. Here, take another twenty. Now you've forty. That'll pay for an imaginary dinner. Good-bye, Colonel! I have an engagement—to meet some of your cavalry. Remember, Morgan's guerrillas are not rascals, but gentlemen. Good-bye!" He vanished.

About noon those of us who appeared unable to march farther were put on top of freight cars, and carried about a dozen miles east to Waynesboro. Here the railway crosses a stream, which encircles a little island just north of the bridge. The majority had to walk. At dusk that Sunday evening all had come. They put us on the island carefully guarded on all sides. Never was I more thankful. I had had something good to eat at Staunton; had got rested riding on the roof of the car; and I had my overcoat. Davy Crockett preferred a heap of chestnut burs for a pillow; but I followed the patriarch's example and chose a flat stone. People never allowed me to sing; but I dropped asleep repeating the stanza in Mrs. Adams's exquisite hymn.

Though, like the wanderer,
    The sun gone down,
Darkness be over me,
    My rest a stone,
Yet in my dreams I'd be
Nearer, my God, to thee!

Towards midnight the cold became so keen that I rose and went to the side of a flickering fire. Here excessive misery was for a moment hardening the hearts it should have softened. Several prisoners were quarreling for a position nearest the embers, each angrily claiming that he had brought the fagots that were burning! Two or three hours later several of us attempted to slip past the sentries in the darkness, but were stopped before we reached the water.

At earliest streak of dawn we were marched away. About two miles brought us to the Blue Ridge where the railroad tunnel pierces its foundations. We toiled up and on in time to see the sun rise. An ocean of fog lay around us. Never shall we forget how royally the King of Day scaled the great wall that seemed to hem in on every side the wide valley, and how the sea of mist and cloud visibly fled before the inrolling flood of light, unveiling green and yellow fields, flocks and herds, dark woodlands, dwellings yet asleep in peace and plenty, here and there the silver thread of a winding stream with lakes that mirrored the sky, and yonder the long stretches of those titanic fortifications encompassing all. We were reminded of Shakespeare's sunrise:

> Full many a glorious morning have I seen
> Flatter the mountain tops with sovereign eye,
> Kissing with golden face the meadows green,
> Gilding pale streams with heavenly alchemy.

At that instant a train of cars from Charlottesville came sliding along, and shot

> Into the tunnel, like a lightning wedge
> By great Thor hammers driven through the rock!

The scene startled us by its sublimity, and for a few minutes the hungry forgot their craving, the footsore their pain, the hopeless their despair.

That day's march, though not so long was as severe as any; we were exhausted. Private Dolan, Co. K, 159th N. Y., was barefoot. His feet were blistered and bleeding. I begged the commander of the provost guard, Captain Haslett, to allow him to get into an ambulance. My request was not granted. But we soon afterwards passed a large mansion in front of which were several girls and women apparently making fun of the unwashed "Yank" and evidently enjoying the spectacle. We were halted just as Dolan came limping along supported on one side by a stronger comrade. They saw his miserable plight, his distress, his swollen feet, and they heard of the stern command to shoot any prisoner who fell out or lagged behind. Their faces changed. With tears one or two implored the Captain to let him ride in the ambulance. He yielded to their entreaties. Southern ladies almost always seemed handsome to us, but these in my memory have the fairest faces. I thought of Lady Clare in *Marmion*, and the words still recur:

O Woman! in our hours of ease,
Uncertain, coy, and hard to please,
And variable as the shade
By the light quivering aspen made;
When pain and anguish wring the brow,
A ministering angel thou!

Two miles before we reached our temporary destination, Meacham's Station, my own strength utterly failed. I had borne up so long, partly to set an example of cheerful endurance, and partly from something like Mark Tapley's pride at coming out strong and jolly under the most depressing circumstances. I lay beside the road, remarking to Captain Haslett, who immediately came riding to the spot, "Captain, here's a fine chance to try your marksmanship; I can't march any further; shan't try to."—"Colonel," he replied with something of pity in his tone and manner, "I'm sorry to see you so used up. I'm sorry to be obliged to march you prisoners so hard. I have to keep out of the way of your damned cavalry. You may get into the ambulance." So into the ambulance I climbed with some difficulty, and immediately commenced my freemasonry on the driver. He responded to the signs. He proved to be an acquaintance of the Redwoods, a family in Mobile, one of whom had been a classmate of mine at Yale. He gave me some nice milk and some fine wheat bread. "As a Mason," said he, "I'll feed you; share the last crumb with you; but as a Confederate soldier I'll fight you till the last drop of blood and the last ditch."—"I hardly know which to admire most, your spunk or your milk," I replied. Thereupon he gave me another drink, and insisted on my imbibing a little of what he called "apple-jack." I was a "teetotaler"; but thinking the occasion warranted, I "smiled" upon it, "strictly as a medicine!" "Apple-jack" seemed to me the same thing as "Jersey lightning." He became quite friendly, but was horribly profane. "Look here," said he, "you seem to be a sort of Christian; cuss me if you don't! What in h—l are you Yanks all comin' down here for?"—"You have a gift at swearing," I said; "did you, among your other oaths, ever swear to support the Constitution of the United States?"—"Well, yes."—"That's what's the matter with us," I said, "we're keeping our oaths and you are breaking yours."—"To h—l with the Constitution of the United States! Our first duty is to our own State. We've a right to be an independent nation, and we will. I'm a guerrilla. If our armies are defeated, I'll fight you on my own hook. I'll fire on you from behind every tree and every rock. I'll assassinate every invader. I want you to remember that I'm a guerrilla."—"I like your *spirits*," I said. "They are worthy of a better cause."—"Take another swallow of 'em," he replied, handing me the canteen. I toasted him: "Here's hoping you gorillas will outlive the Southern Confederacy!"—"A d—d equivocal sentiment," observed my fire-eating, fire-drinking Masonic brother; "but here we are at Meacham's Station. Good-bye, Yank!"

After our nineteen miles' march it was a most welcome relief to be placed on platform cars, though packed so closely that we could hardly stir. We objected that the cars had no tops. "All the better opportunity to study astronomy," they replied.—"The cars have no sides to keep off the wind."—"The scenery is magnificent," they rejoined, "and they'll answer for 'observation cars'; you have an unobstructed view."—"But the nights are growing cold."—"You'll keep warm by contact with each other." Mad at this mockery, hungry, half-frozen, squeezed like fish in a basket, we took little note of scenery or stars; but it was a comfort to believe that our discomfort was caused by the rapid advance of Sheridan's cavalry.

More dead than alive, though hardly dead enough to bury, having been jolted along all the afternoon and all night, we reached Richmond about sunrise, Tuesday, September 27th. Numbering now nearly four hundred we were escorted through the streets to the notorious Libby prison and halted in front. The Union officers inside thronged the windows to see us come. On every face was a sad, despondent, pitying look, the most discouraging sight I ever saw. No smiles there nor among us. Conspicuous among them was the sorrowful countenance of Lieut.-Col. Charles H. Hooper of the 24th Massachusetts Infantry, with his long handsome auburn beard. Some one inside whispered loud enough for several of our "Four Hundred" to hear, "Hide your greenbacks!" We passed the word down the column, "Hide your greenbacks!"

A few minutes revealed its significance. We were taken in a body in upon the lower floor. There Major Nat. Turner, prison inspector, cousin of the celebrated Dick Turner of unlovely reputation, made us a speech.

> You will empty your pockets of all valuables. Such as are not contraband of war, you will be allowed to retain. You will deliver up all your Federal money. An equivalent amount in Confederate money will be given you in instalments from time to time, or the whole will be returned to you when you are exchanged. You will turn pockets inside out. If you attempt to conceal anything, it will be confiscated.

We were made to step forward singly, and were searched. Our coats and vests were taken off, also our boots and shoes; and a Confederate officer felt very carefully of all our clothing to make sure that nothing was hidden. I "remembered to forget" that I had two ten-dollar greenbacks compressed into a little wad in one corner of my watch fob; and that corner escaped inspection. Dick Turpin never was the richer for that money. They examined suspiciously a pocket edition of the New Testament in the original Greek; but I assured them it was not some diabolical Yankee cipher, and they allowed me to keep it. I made the most of my freemasonry, and they permitted me to retain my overcoat. One of our prisoners, it was whispered, had secretly stuffed $1300 in greenbacks into his canteen, but all canteens were taken from us as contraband of war, and nobody but "Uncle Sam" profited by the concealment.

Having "gone through" us, they incarcerated the officers in one room, the enlisted men in another.

FOOTNOTES:

[4] Dr. Fontleroy was a brother of Mrs. Major Whittlesey, one of my fellow professors, instructor in military tactics, at Cornell University. Whittlesey was a graduate of West Point, and, while there, had had cadet U. S. Grant under his command!

CHAPTER IV

At Libby—Thence to Clover, Danville, Greensboro, and Salisbury —Effort to Pledge us not to Attempt Escape.

THE two rooms at Libby adjoined each other on the second floor, but a solid brick wall was between them. When we entered, about a hundred and fifty officers were already there. The first thing that attracted my attention was an officer putting a loaf of bread through a small hole in the partition where one or two bricks were removable. He was feeding a hungry prisoner. A cap or hat nicely concealed the perforation.

Libby has a hard name, but it was the most comfortable of the six Confederate prisons of which I saw the interior. With all his alleged brutal severity, of which I saw no manifestation, and his ravenous appetite for greenbacks, for which we could not blame him, Dick Turner seemed an excellent disciplinarian. Everything went like clockwork. We knew what to expect or rather what not to expect, and *when*! My diary for Wednesday, September 28, 1864, the day after our arrival, reads as follows:

> The issue to us daily is
> One gill of boiled beans,
> One quarter gill of bean broth,
> One half loaf of soft bread,
> (Four ounces meat) and
> A little salt.

There was one inestimable boon, a copious supply of pure water.

There were at this time no panes of glass, in fact no sashes, in the windows, and the wind swept freely through. The nights were becoming cold. Confederate sentries were on the lower floor and outside. They kept up a custom rather unusual, I think, during the war, of calling out in sing-song tones every hour the number of the post and the time, with occasional variations; *e. g.*: "Post number fourteen, two o'clock, and all's well." Then the next sentinel would sing out, "Post number fifteen, two o'clock, and all's well." Then the melodious voice of the next, farther away and sadly unorthodox, "Post number sixteen, two o'clock, and cold as h—l!"

Except one or two rickety tables and two or three old chairs, there was no furniture in the prison. Some of the officers had contrived to save a little money when searched, and with money it was possible to procure small articles slyly smuggled in contrary to orders; but most of us were disposed to sing with old Isaac Watts,

Dear Lord, and shall we ever live
At this poor dying rate?

From the rear windows we were occasionally entertained with the sight of exploding shells, which the indefatigable Grant was daily projecting towards Richmond. Particularly was this the case on the thirtieth of the month, when the boys in blue captured Fort Harrison, and the next day when the Confederates made several gallant but unsuccessful attempts to retake it. At such times we could see some of the steeples or high roofs in Richmond thronged with non-combatants gazing anxiously towards Petersburg. The belief that our prison was undermined, a vast quantity of gunpowder stored in the cellar, and that Dick Turner had threatened and was desperate enough to blow us all into eternity in case of a sudden dash of our cavalry into Richmond, somewhat marred the satisfaction with which we contemplated the evident progress of the siege. We could sympathize with the Philadelphia Friend, who said to his wife on the introduction of gun-cotton, "What comfort can thee take, even when sitting in thy easy chair, when thee knows not but the very cushion underneath thee is an enormous bomb-shell, ready upon the slightest concussion to blow thee to everlasting glory?"

At three o'clock, Sunday morning, October 2d, we were roused by the entry of armed men with lanterns. They furnished each of us with a dirty haversack containing what they called two days' rations of corn bread and meat. Then they moved us single-file down stairs. As we passed, they took from each his blanket, even those the officers had just bought and paid for. If we expostulated, we were told we were going to a place where we should not need blankets! For my freemasonry or some other unexpressed reason, they allowed me to pass, wearing my overcoat. Then they took us by bridge across the James River, packed us in box-cars on the railway, forty to sixty in each car, and started the train southwest towards Danville.

The road-bed was bad and the fences on either side were gone. We made but four or five miles an hour. One of our officers declared that they kept a boy running ahead of the engine with hammer and nails to repair the track! also that they put the cow-catcher on behind the last car to prevent cattle from running over the train! At nine o'clock in the evening we reached a place called Clover. We passed the night in Clover! on the bank beside the railroad, where we studied astronomy! and meditated!

Next morning they repacked us, and we were transported seventy miles farther to Danville. My memorandum book mentions a conversation I had on the way with a very young and handsome rebel, one of the guard. He was evidently ingenuous and sincere, pious and lovable. After a few pleasant remarks he suddenly asked:

"What are you Northerners fighting for?"

"In defense of the Constitution and the Union. What are *you* fighting for?"

"Every right that is sacred and dear to man."

"What right that is sacred and dear to man had the United States ever violated before you fired on Fort Sumter?"

Of course he fell back on the Declaration of American Independence, that "Governments derive their just powers from the consent of the governed"; also on the doctrine so emphatically expressed by Abraham Lincoln in his speech in Congress in 1846; viz.:

> Any people anywhere, being inclined and having the power, have the right to raise up and shake off the existing government, and form a new one that suits them better. This is a most valuable, a most sacred right, a right which we hope and believe is to liberate the world. Nor is this right confined to cases in which the whole people of an existing government may choose to exercise it. Any portion of such

people, that can, may revolutionize and make their own of as much territory as they inhabit.

We arrived at Danville at noon. A heavy rain began to fall. Having been two days without opportunity to wash, we were drenched for an hour or two by the sweet shower that seemed to pour from the open windows of heaven. When our thoughtful guards concluded that we were sufficiently cleansed and bleached, they sheltered us by putting us into coal cars, where the black dust was an inch deep. That dust was fine! but the thought seemed to strike them that our nicely laundered garments might get soiled. So in half an hour they took us out and placed us in corn cars. It rather went against the grain, but finally I sat down with the other kernels on the floor. The weather being inclement, they felt it their duty to keep us in doors, lest we should catch cold!

In these elegant and commodious vehicles we were transported next day till we reached Greensboro, North Carolina, about fifty miles southwest from Danville. Disgorged like poor old Jonah after three days' living burial, we were placed in the beautiful open square, and never before did air, earth, trees, and skies seem lovelier. Here they gave each of us three horny crackers, "rebel hardtack," out of which some of us carved finger rings that might have passed for bone.

In those days I was too much addicted to making public speeches, a habit which I had contracted in Yale College. On the edge of the public green, backed by a hundred prisoners, I was haranguing a crowd of curious spectators, telling them how abominably we were treated, exhibiting to them our single ration of flinty biscuit, and consigning them all to everlasting perdition, when a well-dressed young man elbowed his way to me at the fence. He had a large black shiny haversack swung under his left arm. Patting it with his right hand, he asked:

"Will you have a snack?"

"A what?" I answered.

"A snack, a snack," he said.

"I don't know what a 'snack' is, unless it's a *snake*. Yes, I think I could eat a copperhead—*cooked*. Snake for one, if you please; well done."

He thrust his hand into his haversack; took out and gave me the most delicious sandwich I ever tasted. Seeing how I enjoyed it, he emptied the satchel, giving all his food to my hungry fellow prisoners. He told me he was just starting on a long journey, and had laid in a good stock of provisions. I took pains to write in my journal his name and residence —"George W. Swepson, Alamance, North Carolina. Lives near the Court House." To which I added "*Vir et Amicus*."—"The blessing of him that was ready to perish" was upon George W. Swepson.

That night we slept again on the ground and without covering under the open sky; and again several prisoners, Captain Howe and myself among them, attempted in vain to slip past the sentinels.

Next morning we reëntered the freight cars. A twelve hours' ride brought us at nine o'clock, Wednesday evening, October 5th, to our destination, Salisbury, North Carolina. As the "Four Hundred" passed into the dark enclosure, we were greeted with the cry, "Fresh fish! Fresh fish!" which in those days announced the arrival of a new lot of prisoners. We field officers were quartered that night in a brick building near the entrance, where we passed an hour of horrors. We were attacked by what appeared to be an organized gang of desperadoes, made up of thieves, robbers, Yankee deserters, rebel deserters, and villains generally, maddened by hunger, or bent on plunder, who rejoiced in the euphonious appellation of *Muggers*! We had been warned against them by kindly disposed guards, and were not wholly unprepared. They attacked us with clubs, fists, and knives, but were repeatedly driven off, pitched headlong downstairs. "*Muggers!*"

Salisbury prison, then commonly called "Salisbury penitentiary," was in the general form of a right-angled triangle with base of thirty or forty rods, perpendicular eighty or ninety. In a row parallel to the base and four or five rods from it were four empty log houses with a space of about four rods between each two. These, a story and a half high, had formerly been negro quarters. On each side of the great triangle was a stout tight board fence twelve or fifteen feet high. Some two or three feet from the top of this, but out of our sight because on the other side, there was evidently a board walk, on which sentinels, four or five rods apart, perpetually paced their beats, each being able to see the whole inside of the enclosure. At each angle of the base was a shotted field-piece pointing through the narrow opening. We could see that behind each cannon there was a number of muskets stacked and vigilant soldiers watching every movement inside. Close to the fence outside there were three camps of Confederates, variously estimated to contain from seven hundred to two thousand in all.

The number of Union officers in prison after our arrival was about three hundred and twenty; the number of non-commissioned officers and privates was suddenly increased from about two thousand to some eight thousand. Among these were non-combatants, refugees, lighthouse keepers, and other government employees. Albert D. Richardson, then well-known as a correspondent of the New York *Tribune*, whose romantic marriage to Abby Sage by Henry Ward Beecher and whose tragic death created a sensation in the newspaper world, had been held as a prisoner there for several months. He told us he had found Salisbury a comfortable place. It immediately ceased to be such.

There stood the empty log houses. We besought the rebel commandant, Major Gee, to allow us officers to occupy those buildings. He said he would permit it on condition that we should sign a stringent parole, binding us on our honor not to attempt to escape! We objected to it as a preposterous requirement that, remaining under strict guard and wholly cut off from communication with the outside world, we should sign such a pledge as the only condition on which we could receive decent shelter. I asked Major Gee if the rigor of our confinement would be in any way relaxed. He answered bluntly, "No."—"Well, where's the reciprocity?" I demanded; "what are you giving up?"—"Well," he replied, "if you don't choose to sign the parole, you can't have the buildings. Other Federal officers have not objected to signing it." He showed us the signature of Gen. Michael Corcoran, who had been colonel of the 69th New York, was captured at the first battle of Bull Run, was promoted to be brigadier, and who raised the so-called "Corcoran Legion." Our senior officer, Brig.-Gen. Joseph Hayes of the Fifth Corps, now called a meeting of the field officers, and submitted the question, "Shall we sign the parole, and so obtain shelter? Or shall we hold ourselves free to escape if we can, and so share the privations of our enlisted men, who have no bed but the ground and no covering but the sky?" I spoke strongly against making any promise. We voted almost unanimously against it.

General Hayes and others then urged upon the commandant the absurdity and meanness of requiring it. It was clear to us and must have been so to him that it was for his interest to separate the three or four hundred officers from the thousands of prisoners accustomed to obey our orders. He finally consented that we should occupy the houses without imposing any conditions.

Parallel to the front of these buildings, about five rods from them and extending across the enclosure, was a so-called "dead line," on which nine sentinels paced their beats. Another "dead line" about four rods from the high fence paralleled the whole length of each side of the prison. It was death to come near these.

About eighty officers were assigned to each of the four houses. In each an officer was elected to serve as house-commissary. His duty was to receive the rations from Lieutenant-Colonel Hooper, already mentioned, acting as commissary-general, to whom the Confederate authorities delivered them in bulk. The house-commissary distributed the food and acted as agent representing the house in all communications with Confederate headquarters. Col. Gilbert G. Prey of the 104th N. Y. Vols. was elected commissary of house number one; Capt. D. Tarbell, of Groton, N. Y., commissary of house number two; Lieutenant Reilly of Philadelphia, of house number three; and I of house four.

Each house contained but two rooms, a lower and an upper, both empty, for the most part without glass windows or even sashes; the spaces between the crooked logs not stopped up; a single fireplace in each house, but not half enough wood to keep a blaze; without tables, benches, or chairs; without cooking utensils; without table, knife, fork, spoon, or plate; often without cup or dish; without blankets, or any clothing but the scantiest summer outfit; without books or papers; without water sufficient for washing, or soap, if we could possibly get water; we were in a sorry plight as the nights grew colder. And if the prospect was bad for us, how much worse for our soldiers across the "dead line," who had no shelter, hardly a scrap of blanket! Every rain made their beds a pool or mass of mire. It is not pleasant, but it is a duty to record some of the shadows of our prison life, "lest we forget."

On the open ground outside of what was called the "hospital," October 8th, a sergeant-major was found dead; October 9th, two private soldiers; October 13th, five; October 14th, two; October 16th, eleven; October 17th, seven; October 18th, nine. We could tell how severe the weather had been at night by the number found dead in the morning.

Not far from the prison enclosure was an abundance of growing timber. More than once I besought Major Gee to allow our men to go, under guard on parole, to get wood for fires and for barracks. He refused. He said he was intending to build barracks for the prisoners as soon as he could procure lumber. I presume that he was sincere in this. I asked in vain for blankets for the men; for tents, but none came till December, and then but one "Sibley" tent and one "A" tent per hundred prisoners, not enough for one-third of them.

We procured water from a deep well on the grounds. The supply was so scanty for the thousands of prisoners that it was always exhausted before sunrise. Soon after we came the Confederates commenced digging two new wells. At their rate of progress we reckoned it would take several months to finish either.

My memorandum book shows that the issue of food daily at Salisbury, though sometimes partly withheld, was for each prisoner "one half loaf of soft bread; two, three, four, or five ounces of meat; a gill of boiled rice, and a little salt." I have no doubt that Major Gee meant to deal fairly with us; but he was unprepared for the avalanche that had descended upon him. We are too much in the habit of blaming individual combatants for severities and cruelties that are inherent in the whole business of war, either civil or international, and inseparable from it. Said our Lieut.-Gen. S. M. B. Young at a banquet in Philadelphia, "War is necessarily cruel; it is kill and burn, and burn and kill, and again kill and burn." The truth was more bluntly expressed by the British Rear-Admiral Lord Fisher, now the first sea lord of the British Admiralty:

> Humanizing war? [said he]; you might as well talk of humanizing hell! When a silly ass got up at the first Hague Peace Conference in 1899, and talked about the "amenities of warfare" and putting your prisoners' feet in warm water

> and giving them gruel, my reply, I regret to say, was considered brutally unfit for publication. As if war could be "civilized"! If I am in command when war breaks out, I shall issue as my orders, "The essence of war is violence. Moderation is imbecility. *Hit first, hit hard, hit everywhere.*"

In this light we may view more charitably the slaying, on the 16th of October at Salisbury, of Second Lieutenant John Davis of the 155th N. Y. It was a Sunday morning about half-past ten o'clock. One of our fellow prisoners, Rev. Mr. Emerson, chaplain of a Vermont regiment, had circulated notice that he would conduct religious services in the open air between houses number three and four. The officers were beginning to assemble when the sharp report of a musket near by was heard. Rushing to the spot, we found the lieutenant lying on his back dying at the "dead line." The sentinel on the fence, a mere boy, had fired upon him, and was now reloading. One of our number, Captain William Cook, unable to restrain his anger, hurled a large stone at him. But the hundreds of Confederates in the camps just beyond the fence had sprung to arms at the sound of the firing; the top of the fence was being lined with soldiers; and the vigilant cannoneers at the angles were training their artillery upon our dense mass of officers. We prisoners regarded the shooting as a brutal murder. The religious exercises were turned into a funeral service. Chaplain Emerson prayed, "O God! our only refuge in this dark hour, avenge the atrocious murder of our beloved comrade; protect that widow so cruelly robbed of one dearer to her than life; and especially grant that this accursed Confederacy may speedily sink into its native hell!" His text was from *Isaiah* viii, 12: "Say ye not a Confederacy!" Next day I asked the officer of the guard if any punishment was to be inflicted upon the sentinel. He answered: "No; we don't punish men for doing their duty."

So vitally important is the point of view in deciding upon the right or wrong of an act.

CHAPTER V

At Salisbury—Great Plot to Escape—How Frustrated.

When we arrived at Salisbury early in October, we found there a brave and sagacious officer, Lieut. Wm. C. Manning of the 2d Massachusetts Cavalry. He told us he had been held as a hostage in solitary confinement, and would have starved but for the rats he caught and ate. He had been notified that his own life depended upon the fate of a person held in federal hands as a spy. He determined to attempt an escape. He was assigned to my house. Taking up a part of the floor, he commenced digging a tunnel. He wrote a solemn pledge which all the officers in the house signed, binding them not to divulge the scheme. The tunnel would have had to be about eight rods long, and its outlet would necessarily have been near a group of rebel tents. Of course it would have been discovered on the morning after its completion, and not all could hope to find egress that way. But he believed that his life was still in special danger, and he at once began excavating. The house had no cellar, but there was plenty of room under it for stowing away the loose earth. The ground was not hard, yet it was quite firm, and on the whole favorable for such operations. The work was progressing finely, till the officers were suddenly removed from Salisbury in consequence of the discovery of a great plot.

I had become a good deal interested in Manning and his tunnel plan, and on the morning of Wednesday, October 12th, I introduced him to General Hayes, our senior officer. He told us he had for several days been considering the possibility of organizing the three or four hundred officers, and the five to ten thousand soldiers. He believed that by a simultaneous assault at many points we could seize the artillery, break the fence, capture the three rebel camps, then arm and ration this extemporized army, and march away. He showed us a good map of North Carolina. He invited all of the field officers to meet that evening in the garret of house number two. All of them accordingly, about thirty in number, were present. Posting sentinels to keep out intruders, and stopping the open windows so that the faint light of a tallow candle might not betray us or create suspicion, we sat down in the gloom.

The general had modestly absented himself, in order that we might be uninfluenced by him in reaching a decision; but our first step was to send for him, and then insist on his taking the chair—*the* chair, for we had but one! As he had made a careful study of the subject, we pressed him to give his views. He proceeded to state the grounds of his belief that it was practicable to strike an effective blow for our liberation. He told us that he had communicated with a Union man outside, and had learned the number and location of the Confederate troops we should be likely to encounter on our march to East Tennessee. He explained at some length the details of his plan, the obstacles we should encounter, and how to overcome them. I shall never forget the conclusion of his speech. These were almost exactly his words:

> We must organize; organize victory. The sooner we act the better, provided we have a well-arranged plan. We can capture this town, ration our men, provide them with shoes, clothing, and muskets, and have a formidable army right here at once. It need not take more than half a day. Certainly we can march off within twenty-four hours after the first blow is struck, if we begin right. The enemy have a few guns on the hill, but they are not "in battery". We can take these and take the artillery here right along with us. The principal obstacle is here; make the beginning right; master these prisons and these camps, and we are safe. Organize is the word; *organize*. If any one shall betray us, or aid the rebels, or be guilty of robbery or other outrage, I am in favor of a drumhead court martial and a summary execution. Now, gentlemen, I am ready to serve in any capacity, whether to lead or to follow.

Colonel Ralston of the 24th N. Y. "dismounted cavalry," as they were called, spoke next. He was an energetic and dashing officer who fell near me in an attempt to break out of Danville prison on the tenth of the following December. He entered into the particulars of a plan of action, showing how easy it would be, with the probable loss of but few lives, to capture the three camps with the Salisbury arsenal and the artillery. As his particular share in the work, he said he would undertake with a small company to disarm the twenty or thirty sentinels inside the enclosure, and instantly thereupon to capture the headquarters of Major Gee.

Other officers gave valuable suggestions. Being called upon for my opinion, I spoke of the duty we owed our enlisted men to extricate them from their shocking condition, for they were beginning to die every night on the bare ground, and would soon be perishing by scores. I urged the effect the escape of some eight thousand prisoners would have upon the nation, being equivalent to a great victory; and, better than victory, it would add so many thousands of trained soldiers at once to our armies in the field. I insisted that this success would be cheaply bought, even if it cost, as it probably would, a hundred lives.

Of all our thirty field officers, only one opposed the scheme (Lieut.-Col. G——). He was acknowledged to be brave,[5] but seemingly lacking in enterprise. He said in substance, "I have carefully examined the situation, and have come to the conclusion that it is utterly useless to attempt to escape by force. It can't be done at present. We should be slaughtered by the hundred. If you all vote to try it, I will join you; but in my opinion it is perfect madness."

With but one dissenting voice it was resolved to go ahead. A committee of five was immediately appointed to prepare and present a plan of action. This committee were Colonel Ralston; Col. W. Ross Hartshorne, 190th Pa. (the famous "Bucktail Regiment," whose first colonel, O'Neil, my Yale classmate, was killed at Antietam); Col. James Carle, 191st Pa.; Major John Byrne, 155th N. Y.; and myself, Lieutenant-Colonel of the 13th Conn. We were supposed to be fighting men, and had all been wounded in battle.

A similar meeting of field officers was held the following evening. For two days the committee was almost continually in consultation with General Hayes. Great pains was taken to have the plans fully understood by all the officers and to secure their hearty coöperation. By ingenious methods frequent communication was had with the enlisted men across the "dead line"; sometimes by hurling written communications ballasted with stone; several times by Lieutenant Manning and others running swiftly past the sentinels in the dark; best of all, because least liable to discovery, by the use of the deaf-and-dumb alphabet. We were suffering for want of water, and several officers got permission to go outside the enclosure ostensibly to procure it, but really to reconnoitre.

The committee reported the following plan, which was unanimously adopted:

The first object in the movement being to get into a hand-to-hand fight as soon as possible; seven columns, each several hundred strong, were to make simultaneous assaults upon six or seven different points. The fence being the first impediment, every man's haversack and pockets were to be filled with stones to keep down the sentinels who would fire on us from the top. Some got levers to wrench off boards, others logs to serve as rude battering rams, others sharpened stakes which Ralston called "Irish pikes," others clubs, or any possible weapon. I had a rusty old bayonet.

Major David Sadler, 2d Pennsylvania Heavy Artillery, with his battalion was to rush and seize the cannon and muskets at the angle on the right; Major John Byrne and his column at the same instant were to pounce upon the big gun and muskets at the angle on our left; simultaneously Colonel Ralston and his men are to dash upon the nine sentinels on the "dead line" in front of the officers' houses, in a moment disarming them and the nine of the relief just arriving; then spring to the assistance of Major August Haurand of the 4th N. Y. Cavalry and his battalion who are capturing Major Gee's headquarters and guards and camp on our right. Col. James Carle, 191st Pa., with his hundreds is breaking through the fence and capturing the rebel camp in rear of the officers' quarters. Colonel, afterwards General, W. Ross Hartshorne and his 330 men of the 190th Pa. are to break the fence just above the main rebel camp which is on our left. My own column of about three hundred men of the Nineteenth Corps are to break the fence just below the rebel camp; then Hartshorne and I are to leap from opposite sides upon this, the main camp. These seven battalions were to some extent organized with field, staff, and company officers. Every officer and soldier was to be on the *qui vive* a little before five o'clock in the morning, watching intently for the signal. This was to be the waving of a fire-brand by General Hayes in front of house number two.

Quite a number of officers had no faith in the plot, and they regarded it with indifference. A few expressed hostility to it. One captain, who had been a prisoner before and seemed glad to have been captured again, a bloated, overgrown, swaggering, filthy bully, of course a coward, formerly a keeper of a low groggery and said to have been commissioned for political reasons, was repeatedly heard to say in sneering tones in the hearing of rebel sentries, "*Some of our officers have got escape on the brain*," with other words to the like effect. Colonel Hartshorne finally stopped such traitorous language by saying with tremendous emphasis: "Captain D——, I've heard a good deal of your attempts to discourage officers from escaping, and your loud talk about officers having 'escape on the brain.' Now, sir, I give you notice that if you're again guilty of anything of the sort, I'LL—BREAK—YOUR—HEAD—WITH—A—CLUB!"

The time agreed upon for the seven simultaneous attacks was about an hour before sunrise the morning of October 15th.

As we had feared, the rebel authorities, whether through suspected treachery or otherwise, got wind of our purpose. Towards evening of October 14th extraordinary vigilance on their part became apparent. Troops were paraded, posts strengthened, guards doubled, privileges restricted, and word was passed around in our hearing that a battalion of Confederates had just arrived. Their watchfulness seemed unrelaxed through the night. The shooting of Lieutenant Davis next morning was doubtless in obedience to orders for a more rigorous enforcement of rules.

Our outbreak was countermanded and postponed, but preparations continued. The delay enabled us to perfect our plans, and make our organizations more complete. The early morning of October 20th, the 19th being the anniversary of my birth, was now fixed upon for the "insurrection." We essayed to disarm suspicion by an air of quiet acquiescence in the lazy routine of prison life, or absorption in the simplest and most innocent occupations whenever any Confederate might be looking on.

We recognized united and instantaneous action at the signal on the part of three hundred officers and several thousand men as the most vitally important element of success. It was necessary that this should be thoroughly understood and emphasized, so that every soldier should be in perfect readiness at the critical moment.

Several of us had formed a class for oral instruction in French. Our teacher was Captain Cook of the 9th U. S. colored troops, a graduate of Yale. About ten o'clock in the morning of October 18th, as we were seated on the ground near house number four, loudly imitating Professor Cook's *parlez-vous*, Lieut. Wm. C. Gardner, adjutant of one of those extemporized battalions of prisoners, brought me a letter he was intending to throw across the "dead line" to Sergt. Wallace W. Smith, requesting him to notify all enlisted men of the battalion when and where to assemble silently next morning in the dark, how to arm themselves, from whom to take orders, what signal to watch for, and other important matters. I glanced through it, and immediately said: "You'd better not entrust the communication to so hazardous a channel; wait an hour till I've done with my French lesson, and I'll cause it to be transmitted by the deaf-and-dumb alphabet." If I recollect rightly, either Lieutenant Tobey or Lieutenant Morton, both of the 58th Massachusetts, was in the class, and promised to convey the contents of the letter safely across to the soldiers by adroit finger manipulation. We were just finishing the French exercise, when Adjutant Gardner came greatly excited, and this conversation followed:

"Good God, Colonel, the rebs have got that letter! I tied it to a stone and flung it a long ways over the 'dead line' to Wallace Smith. He appeared afraid to pick it up. A reb sentinel stepped away from his beat and got it."

"I requested you to wait till I'd done reciting French, and I told you I'd then communicate it by the deaf-and-dumb alphabet."

"Well, Colonel, I ought to have done so; but I was anxious to have the work done promptly, and I thought it was perfectly safe. I've tossed letters over to Smith several times. I'm worried to death about it. What's best to do?"

"Was your name signed to it?"

"No; but my name was on the envelope—an old letter envelope that I had when we came here."

"Well, Gardner, this is a pretty piece of business! That letter of course will go very soon to Major Gee's headquarters, and then—there'll be the devil to pay!"

"The sentinel handed the letter to the officer of the guard. What had I better say, if they send for me?"

"Say you intended the letter to fall into their hands; that you meant it as a practical joke, wanted to get up another scare, and see the Johnnies prick up their ears again."

"But, Colonel, like a fust-class fool I put a ten-dollar Confederate bill in the envelope. I wanted to give it to Sergeant Smith. That don't look as if I meant it to fall into their hands—does it?"

"Gardner, this thing has an ugly look. You've knocked our plans of escape in the head—at least for the present. You've got yourself into a fix. They'll haul you up to headquarters. They'll prove by the letter that you've been deep in a plot that would have cost a good many lives. They're feeling ugly. They may hang or shoot you before sundown, as a warning to the rest of us to stop these plots to escape. They may send for you at any minute."

"What had I better say or do?"

"You'd better make yourself scarce for a while, till you've got a plausible story made up. Better disguise yourself and pass yourself off as somebody else; so gain time."

"I have it, Colonel; I'll pass myself off as Estabrooks."

Estabrooks was an officer of the 26th Mass., who had escaped at the crossing of the river Yadkin two weeks previously when we came from Richmond. Gardner was a handsome man and perhaps the best-dressed officer in prison; but he now disguised himself.[6] The transformation was complete. In half an hour a man came to me wearing a slouched hat and a very ragged suit of Confederate gray. He had been a play-actor before the war and knew how to conceal his identity. By his voice I recognized him as Gardner! "Well, Gardner," said I, "this surpasses His Satanic Majesty; or, as you would say, beats the devil!"—"Colonel," he replied, "I'm not Gardner.

Gardner escaped; escaped at the crossing of the Yadkin River. I'm Estabrooks, H. L. Estabrooks, 2d Lieutenant, 26th Mass. Call me Estabrooks if you please."—"All right, Estabrooks it is."

Hardly had we had time to whisper around this change of name, when the Confederate officer of the guard made his appearance with two or three soldiers, inquiring for the commissary of house number four. I was pointed out to him. In substance and almost in the exact words this dialogue ensued:

"Colonel Sprague, are you commissary of this house?"

"I have that honor."

"I want to find Lieutenant Gardner."

"Who?"

"Lieutenant Gardner."

"Who's Lieutenant Gardner?"

"I am told he's an officer in house number four; and as you are commissary, you can probably tell me where he is *at*."

"Where he's what?"

"Where he's *at*."

This was the first time I had ever heard the word *at* so used at the end of a sentence; but it expresses the meaning with admirable precision. I had a slight qualm at lying; but I remembered that even George Washington could tell a lie if necessary in war. Pacifying my conscience with the fact that we were *outside* the house at the time, I said:

"There's no such officer in house four. But I remember an officer of that name at Libby, handsomely dressed, a perfect dandy. I heard that he escaped at the crossing of the Yadkin River two weeks ago. Has he been recaptured, and is he going to be shot or hanged? Or have you a letter for him? What's the good news about Gardner?"

"I only know," he replied, "that he's wanted at Major Gee's office, and he's an officer in house number four."

"Estabrooks," said I to the man at my side, "do you know of a Lieutenant Gardner?"

"I did know slightly such a man at Libby. You have described him well; a fop, a beau, a dandy; just about my size, but he didn't wear rags like I do."

"Come with me," said I to the Confederate. "We'll go into the house and inquire if any one knows of a Lieutenant Gardner." We went in. There were perhaps thirty or forty inside who had got wind of what was going on. As we entered, I asked in a loud voice, "Does any officer in this house know anything of a Lieutenant Gardner?" Several smiled and declared it a very singular name. One wanted to know how it was spelled! A number were speaking at once. One said he escaped at the Yadkin; he knew he got away, for he "watched him till he got a long distance out of sight." Another knew a Henry J. Gardner, "a Know-Nothing" governor of Massachusetts, who knew enough to keep out of the army. Another affirmed that Gardner was dead; he had heard him say "I'm a dead man," and he wouldn't tell a lie! My memory is somewhat indistinct of all that was said; but Gardner is alleged to have whispered the officer thus: "I have been a gardener myself; and if Major Gee will parole me and give me good clothes and something to eat, I wouldn't mind becoming again a gardener in his employ." I recollect distinctly that the officer grew impatient and he finally asked me, "Do you say on your honor, Colonel, that you don't know a Lieut. Wm. O. Gardner in this house?" I answered, "I do"; but I left him to guess whether I meant "I do *know*" or "I do *say*!" I quieted my conscientious scruples by remembering that the lieutenant's true name was not Wm. O. but Wm. C.! The baffled officer left very angry, and "*Where's Gardner at?*" passed into a conundrum.

Late that afternoon, as I was engaged in the delightful employment of washing my fall-and-winter shirt, having for the first time since our arrival in Salisbury obtained sufficient water for that purpose, the order came for all officers to fall in and take the cars for Danville, Va. The juxtaposition of three or four hundred Yankee officers with eight thousand of their enlisted comrades-in-arms was getting dangerous.

FOOTNOTES:

[5] He had killed three men with his sword at the time of his capture.

[6] "We run the boy into one of the houses, clipped his hair, shaved him, and placed a new robe on him."—*Letter* of Capt. Wesley C. Howe to Colonel Sprague, Jan. 30, 1914.

CHAPTER VI

From Salisbury to Danville—The Forlorn Situation—Effort to "Extract Sunshine from Cucumbers"—The Vermin—The Prison Commandant a Yale Man—Proposed Theatricals—Rules Adopted—Studies—Vote in Prison for Lincoln and McClellan—Killing Time.

At six o'clock, Wednesday evening, October 19, 1864, we officers, about 350 in number, were packed in five freight cars, and the train was started for Danville, Va. The tops of the cars were covered with armed guards, two or three being also stationed within at the side door of each car. In the darkness about half-past nine Lieut. Joseph B. Simpson of the 11th Indiana slyly stole all the food from the haversacks of the guards at the door of our car and passed it round to us, while we loudly "cussed and discussed" slavery and secession! About midnight Captain Lockwood, Lieutenant Driscoll, and eight or ten other officers leaped from the cars. The guards opened fire upon them. Lockwood was shot dead. Several were recaptured, and some probably reached the Union lines in safety. We arrived at Danville at noon October 20th.

The town at this time contained four, formerly six, military prisons, each a tobacco house about eighty to a hundred feet long by forty to fifty wide, three stories high, built of brick, low between joints. The officers were put into the building known as prison number three. We were informed by the guards that it had formerly contained about two hundred negro prisoners; but that some had died, others had been delivered to their masters or set at work on fortifications, and the number remaining just before our arrival was only sixty-four. These were removed to make room for us.

Except about twenty large stout wooden boxes called spittoons, there was no furniture whatever in prison number three. Conjecture was rife as to the purpose of the Confederates in supplying us with spittoons and nothing else. They were too short for coffins, too large for wash bowls, too shallow for bathing tubs, too deep for tureens! To me much meditating on final causes, a vague suspicion at length arose that there was some mysterious relation between those twenty oblong boxes and a score of hogsheads of plug tobacco, said to be stored in the basement. A *tertium* QUID, a solution of the tobacco, might afford a solution of the spittoon mystery!

A dozen water buckets were put into each of the two upper rooms to which all the officers were restricted; also a small cylinder coal stove; nothing else until December, when another small stove was placed there. Winter came early and unusually cold. The river Dan froze thick. It was some weeks before we prevailed upon the prison commandant to replace with wood the broken-out glass in the upper rooms. The first floor was uninhabitable.

So with no bed nor blanket; no chairs, benches, nor tables; no table-ware nor cooking utensils; not even shovel, poker, or coal-scoop; most of us were in a sorry plight. The little stoves, heated white-hot, would have been entirely inadequate to warm those rooms; but the coal was miserably deficient in quality as well as quantity. The fire often went out. To rekindle it, there was no other way than to upset the whole, emptying ashes and cinders on the floor. At best, the heat was obstructed by a compact ring of shivering officers, who had preëmpted positions nearest the stoves. They had taken upon themselves to "run" the thing; and they did it well. We called them "The Stove Brigade." In spite of their efforts, they like the rest suffered from cold.

Three or four of us, as a sanitary measure, made it a point to see, if possible, the funny, or at least the bright side of everything, turn melancholy to mirth, shadow to sunshine. When every officer complained of cold, we claimed to anticipate the philosophers, Tyndall, Huxley, and the other physicists, in declaring that "heat is a mode of *motion*," and brisk bodily exercise will infallibly demonstrate the fact! When, as was usually the case, all were hungry, we announced as a sure cure for indigestion, "stop *eating*!" When our prisoner chaplain Emerson on a Sunday afternoon prayed for the dear ones we expected to see no more, and even the roughest and most profane were in tears, we said with old Homer, "*Agathoi aridakrues andres*" ("Gallant men are easily moved to tears"), or with Bayard Taylor, "The bravest are the tenderest, the loving are the daring."

Most humiliating of all was the inevitable plague of vermin. "Hard indeed," one officer was accustomed to say, "must have been Pharaoh's heart, and tougher yet his epidermis, if the lice of the third Egyptian plague were like those of Danville, and yet he would not 'let Israel go.'" Wearing the same clothing night and day, sitting on the bare floors, sleeping there in contact with companions not over-nice, no patient labor, no exterminating unguent, afforded much relief. We lost all squeamishness, all delicacy on the subject, all inclination for concealment. It was not a returned Danville prisoner who was reported to have gone into a drug store in New York stealthily scratching and saying, "I want some unguentum; don't want it for myself; only want it for a friend." But it was reported and believed that in April one of them entered an apothecary shop in Annapolis plying his finger-nails and hurriedly asking, "Have you any bmsquintum?"—"From your manner," answered the courteous druggist, "I think what you want is unguentum."—"Yes, *run git 'em*; I guess that *is* the true name."—"Unguentum, sir"; said the shopkeeper. "How much unguentum do you want?"—"Well, I reckon about two pound!"—"My dear sir, two pounds would kill all the lice in Maryland."—"Well, I vow I believe I've got 'em!"

Lieut.-Col. Robert C. Smith of Baltimore, who took command of the Danville prisons soon after our arrival, appeared to be kind-hearted, compassionate, but woefully destitute of what Mrs. Stowe calls "faculty." He was of medium height, spare build, fair complexion, sandy hair, blue eyes, of slightly stooping figure; on the whole rather good-looking. He was slow of speech, with a nasal twang that reminded me of Dr. Horace Bushnell. His face always wore a sad expression. He had been a student at Yale in the forties a few years before me. Once a prisoner himself in our hands and fairly treated, he sympathized with us. He had been wounded, shot through the right shoulder. When I visited on parole the other Danville prisons in February, a Yankee soldier was pointed out to me as wearing Colonel Smith's blood-stained coat, and another was said to be wearing his vest. I had repeated interviews with him, in which he expressed regret at not being able to make us more comfortable. He said more than once to me, "I have no heart for this business. It requires a man without any heart to keep a military prison. I have several times asked to be relieved and sent to the front." An officer of forceful executive ability might have procured for us lumber for benches, more coal or wood for the stoves, some straw or hay for bedding, blankets or cast-off clothing for the half naked; possibly a little food, certainly a supply of reading matter from the charitably disposed. Single instances of his compassion I have mentioned. I shall have occasion to speak of another. But the spectacle of the hopeless mass of misery in the four Danville prisons seemed to render him powerless, if not indifferent. As Mrs. Browning puts it:

A red-haired child,
Sick in a fever, if you touch him once,
Though but so little as with a finger-tip,
Will set you weeping; but a million sick!
You could as soon weep for the rule of three,
Or compound fractions!

Like too many officers both Union and Confederate, he was often in liquor; liquor was always in him. This "knight of the rueful countenance," of the sad heart, the mourning voice, the disabled right arm, and the weakness for apple-jack!—his only hope was to have an exchange of prisoners; but Lincoln and Stanton and Grant would not consent to that. The last I heard of him was when a letter of his was shown me by Lieutenant Washington, a Confederate, a distant relative of the great George. In it Smith, who had been absent a week from Danville, complained that he had had "no liquor for three days," and that he was "painfully sober"!

"Necessity," says the old apothegm, "is the mother of invention." It was surprising, how much we accomplished in a few weeks towards making ourselves comfortable. Bone or wood was carved into knives, forks, spoons, buttons, finger-rings, masonic or army badges, tooth-picks, bosom pins, and other ornaments; corn-cobs were made into smoking pipes; scraps of tin or sheet-iron were fashioned into plates for eating or dishes for cooking; shelves were made by tying long wood splinters together; and many "spittoons," which were soon rendered superfluous, because the two entire rooms were transformed into vast spittoons, were inverted, and made useful as seats which we called sofas.

Many ingeniously wrought specimens of Yankee ingenuity were sold clandestinely to the rebel guards, who ventured to disobey strict orders. No skinflint vender of wooden nutmegs, leather pumpkin-seeds, horn gunflints, shoe-peg oats, huckleberry-leaf tea, bass-wood cheeses, or white-oak hams, ever hankered more for a trade. Besides the products of our prison industry, they craved watches, rings, gold chains, silver spurs, gilt buttons, genuine breast-pins, epaulets; anything that was not manufactured in the Confederacy. Most of all, they longed for greenbacks in exchange for rebel currency. So in one way or another many of us contrived to get a little money of some sort. With it we could buy of the sutler, who visited us from time to time, rice, flour, beans, bacon, onions, dried apple, red peppers, sorghum syrup, vinegar, etc.

Perhaps the best result of our engaging in handicraft work was the relief from unspeakable depression of spirits. Some of us saw the importance of making diversion on a large scale. To this end we planned to start a theatre. Major Wm. H. Fry, of the 16th Pa. Cavalry, who knew all about vaudeville in Philadelphia, was a wise adviser. Young Gardner, who had been an actor, heartily joined in the movement. I procured a worn-out copy of Shakespeare. It seemed best to begin with the presentation of the first act in *Hamlet*. Colonel Smith and other rebel officers promised to aid us. We assigned the parts and commenced studying and rehearsing. Gardner was to be Hamlet; Lieut.-Col. Theodore Gregg, 45th Pa., was to be Claudius, the usurping king; the smooth-faced Capt. William Cook was to be the queen-mother Gertrude; Capt. W. F. Tiemann, 159th N. Y., was to personate Marcellus; Lieut. C. H. Morton of Fairhaven, Mass., I think, was Horatio; and I, having lost about forty pounds of flesh since my capture—it was thought most appropriate that I should be the Ghost! Every morning for some weeks on the empty first floor we read and rehearsed, and really made fine progress. But when we got ready to produce in theatric style, with slight omissions, the first act, the rebels seemed suspicious of some ulterior design. They refused to furnish a sword for Hamlet, a halberd for Marcellus, muskets for Bernardo and Francisco, a calico gown for the queen, or even a white shirt for the Ghost. This was discouraging. When the lovely queen-mother Gertrude appealed to her son—

Good Hamlet, cast thy nighted color off,—

he answered, "I swear I can't do it!" One November morning, as we were rehearsing and shivering on the windy first floor, he ejaculated with some emphasis, and with ungentle expletives not found in the original text,

The air bites shrewdly; it is very cold;

"I move, Colonel, that we 'bust up' this theatre." So the "legitimate drama" vanished from Danville.

About this time my copy of the Greek New Testament was stolen from me, an instance, perhaps, of piety run mad.

A week or two before this, the lower room, in which I then lodged, containing about a hundred and seventy officers, was getting into such a condition that I felt it my duty to call a meeting to see what measures could be adopted to promote comfort and decency. I was not the senior in rank, but Colonel Carle did not feel himself authorized to issue orders. Some sort of government must be instituted at once. Nearly all recognized the necessity of prompt action and strict discipline. A committee was appointed consisting of myself, Major John W. Byron, 88th N. Y., and another officer whose name escapes me, to draw up rules and regulations. We presented the following:

RULES UNANIMOUSLY ADOPTED IN THE LOWER ROOM,
DANVILLE, VA., PRISON, OCT. 26, 1864:

1. The room shall be thoroughly policed (swept, etc.) four times each day by the messes in succession; viz., at sunrise and sunset, and immediately after breakfast and dinner.
2. There shall be no washing in this room.
3. No emptying slops into spittoons.
4. No washing in the soup buckets or water buckets.
5. No shaking of clothes or blankets in this room.
6. No cooking inside the stoves.
7. No loitering in the yard to the inconvenience of others.

8. No person shall be evidently filthy or infested with vermin.
9. No indecent, profane, or ungentlemanly language in this room.
10. No conduct unbecoming an officer and gentleman about these premises.
11. No talking aloud at night after nine o'clock.
12. An officer of the day shall be appointed daily by the senior officer, whose duty shall be to see that these rules are strictly enforced, and to report to the senior officer any violation thereof.
13. In case of any alleged violation of any of these rules, the senior officer of the room shall appoint a Court[7] to consist of thirteen disinterested officers, who shall fairly try and determine the matter, and in case of conviction the offender's rations shall be stopped, or the commander of the prison be requested to confine the offender in a cell according to the sentence of the Court; and it shall be the duty of every officer to have such offender court-martialed after rejoining his command.

For the Committee. H. B. Sprague, Oct, 26, 1864.

The prison commandant promised that he would execute any sentence short of capital punishment. But one case was tried by such court. The offense was a gross violation of rule 9. The culprit was let off with a sharp reprimand by General Hayes; but my first act after the exchange of prisoners was to prefer charges and specifications against him. The beast was court-martialed at Annapolis in the latter part of July, '65.

The observance of these rules wrought wonders in correcting evils which had become almost unendurable, and in promoting cheerfulness, good behavior, and mutual esteem.

Many letters were written to us. Few of them reached their destination. The first I received was from Miss Martha Russell, a lady of fine literary ability, a friend of Edgar A. Poe, living at North Branford, Conn. In raising my company (Co. H., 13th Conn.), I had enlisted her brother Alfred. Under strict military discipline he had become a valuable soldier, and I had appointed him my first sergeant. At the battle of Irish Bend, La., in which I was myself wounded, he was shot through the neck. The wound seemed mortal, but I secured special care for him, and his life was spared as by miracle. His sister's letter brought a ray of sunshine to several of us. It assured us that we were tenderly cared for at home. She quoted to cheer us the fine lines of the Cavalier poet Lovelace,

Stone walls do not a prison make,
Nor iron bars a cage;
Minds innocent and quiet take
That for a hermitage.

A well-grounded conviction prevailed among the prisoners that the Confederate government was anxious to secure an exchange of prisoners, but that the Federal government would not consent. The reason was evident enough. The Confederate prisoners in the North, as a rule, were fit for military duty; the Union prisoners in the South were physically unfit. A general exchange would have placed at once, say, more than forty thousand fresh soldiers in the rebel ranks, but very few in ours. Conscription for military service had been tried in the North with results so bitter that it seemed unwise to attempt it again. Better let the unfortunates in southern prisons perish in silence—that appeared the wisest policy. But to us prisoners it appeared a mistake and gross neglect of duty. Between our keen sense of the wrong in allowing us to starve, and our love for Lincoln and the Union, there was a struggle. Our patriotism was put to the test on the day of the Presidential election, Tuesday, November 8th. Discouraging as was the outlook for us personally, we had confidence in the government and in the justice of our cause. Pains was taken to obtain a full and fair vote in the officers' prison. There were two hundred seventy-six for Lincoln; ninety-one for McClellan. Under the circumstances the result was satisfactory.

Very earnest, if not acrimonious, were the discussions that immediately preceded and followed. Some of us realized their importance, not so much in arriving at a correct decision on the questions at issue, as in preventing mental stagnation likely to result in imbecility if not actual idiocy. By the stimulus of employment of some kind we must fight against the apathy, the hopeless loss of will power, into which several of our comrades seemed sinking. Mrs. Browning well says:

Get leave to work
In this world,—'tis the best you get at all.
... Get work; get work;
Be sure 'tis better than what you work to get!

Some of us started historical debates, and new views were presented which furnished both amusement and instruction. One colonel, more redoubtable in battle than in dialectics, who had been shot through from breast to back, gravely informed us that the geometer Euclid was an early English writer! A kindly visitor, Dr. Holbrook, made me a present of Hitchcock's *Elementary Geology*. It was not quite up to date, having been published about twenty-five years before, but I found the study interesting. Grieved at having lost from my books three years in military service, I endeavored with three or four companions to make up for the deficiency by taking lessons in French. Our teacher was Captain Cook, already mentioned as teaching us French at Salisbury. As we had no books, the instruction was oral. I was delighted to observe how much a knowledge of Latin facilitated the acquisition of the modern tongue. A few weeks later upon the arrival of Major George Haven Putnam, Adjutant at that time of the 176th N. Y., several of us commenced under him the study of German. Here too the teaching was oral; but I was able to buy Oehlschläger's *German Reader*; took special pleasure in memorizing some of the selections, particularly from the poets Gleim, Claudius, Goethe, Schiller, and Uhland; and I was already familiar with some stanzas of Arndt's noble *The German Fatherland*, sung so often to me by my Lieutenant Meisner, slain by my side in battle. Some of those songs still ring in my ears. General Hayes, Major Putnam, and two or three others took lessons in Spanish from a native of Mexico, 2d Lieut. John Gayetti (I think that was his name), of Battery B, 2d Pa. Artillery.

Checkerboards and chessboards were prepared from the rudest materials, and many were the games with which some of our comrades sought to beguile the weary hours. Capt. Frank H. Mason of the 12th Cavalry had the reputation of being our best chess player and young Adjutant Putnam was his most persistent opponent.

No one needs to be told that old soldiers are great story-tellers, drawing upon their imagination for facts. This talent was assiduously cultivated in our prison.

FOOTNOTES:

[7] See Appendix.

CHAPTER VII

Exact Record of Rations in Danville—Opportunity to Cook—Daily Routine of Proceedings from Early Dawn till Late at Night.

Our imprisonment at Danville lasted from October 20, '64, to February 17, '65, one hundred and twenty days. I kept a careful daily record of the rations issued to us, as did also Lieut. Watson W. Bush, 2d N. Y. "Mounted Rifles." After our removal from Danville to Richmond for exchange, we compared our memoranda, and found they substantially agreed. During the one hundred and twenty days the issues were as follows:

> *Bread.* A loaf every morning. It was made of unsifted corn-meal, ground "cobs and all." Pieces several inches in length of cobs unground were sometimes contained in it. It always seemed wholesome, though moist, almost watery. Its dimensions were a little less than 7 inches long, 3 or 4 wide, and 3 thick. I managed to bring home a loaf, and we were amazed at the shrinkage to a quarter of its original size. It had become very hard. We broke it in two, and found inside what appeared to be a dishcloth!
>
> *Meat.* Forty-three times. I estimated the weight at from 2 to 5 or 6 ounces. In it sometimes were hides, brains, heads, tails, jaws with teeth, lights, livers, kidneys, intestines, and nameless portions of the animal economy.
>
> *Soup.* Sixty-two times; viz., bean soup forty-seven times; cabbage nine times; gruel six. It was the thinnest decoction of small black beans, the slightest infusion of cabbage, or the most attenuated gruel of corn-cob meal, that a poetic imagination ever dignified with the name of *soup*!
>
> *Potatoes.* Seven times. Seldom was one over an inch in diameter.

Salt fish. Five times. They call it "hake." It was good. "Hunger the best sauce."

Sorghum syrup. Three times. It was known as "corn-stalk molasses." It was not bad.

Nothing else was given us for food by the Confederates at Danville. The rations appeared to deteriorate and diminish as the winter advanced. My diary shows that in the fifty-three days after Christmas we received meat only three times.

Manifestly such supplies are insufficient to sustain life very long. By purchase from the rebel sutler who occasionally visited us, or by surreptitious trading with the guards, we might make additions to our scanty allowance. I recollect that two dollars of irredeemable treasury notes would buy a gill of rice or beans or corn, a turnip, onion, parsnip, or small pickled cucumber!

The Confederate cooking needed to be supplemented. Here the cylinder coal-stoves were made useful. The tops of them were often covered with toasting corn bread. Tin pails and iron kettles of various capacities, from a pint to several quarts, suspended from the top by wooden hooks a foot or two in length, each vessel resting against the hot stove and containing rice, beans, Indian corn, dried apple, crust coffee, or other delicacy potable or edible slowly preparing, made the whole look like a big black chandelier with pendants. We were rather proud of our prison cuisine. Cooking was also performed on and in an old worn-out cook-stove, which a few of our millionaires, forming a joint-stock company for the purpose, had bought for two hundred Confederate dollars late in the season, and which the kind prison commander had permitted them to place near the southwest end of the upper room, running the pipe out of a window. Culinary operations were extensively carried on also in the open yard outside, about forty feet by twenty, at the northeast end of the building. Here the officer would build a diminutive fire of chips or splinters between bricks, and boil or toast or roast his allowance. We were grouped in messes of five to ten or twelve each. Happy the club of half a dozen that could get money enough and a big enough kettle to have their meal prepared jointly.

Such was the case with my own group after the lapse of about two months. We had been pinched; but one morning Captain Cook came to me with radiant face and said: "Colonel, I have good news for you. *I*'m going to run this mess. My folks in New York have made arrangement with friends in England to supply me with money, and I've just received through the lines a hundred dollars. We'll live like fighting-cocks!" Adjt. J. A. Clark, 17th Pa. Cav., was our delighted cook. Shivering for an hour over the big kettle amid the ice and snow of the back yard, he would send up word, "Colonel, set the table for dinner." To "set the table" consisted in sweeping a space six or eight feet square, and depositing there the plates, wood, tin, or earthen (mine was of wood; it had cost me a week's labor in carving). The officers already mentioned, Cook, Clark, Bush, Sprague, with Lieut. E. H. Wilder, 9th N. Y. Cav., sit around in the elegant Turkish fashion, or more classical recline like the ancients in their symposia, each resting on his left elbow, with face as near as possible to the steaming kettle, that not a smell may be lost!

Wood was scarce. It was used with most rigid economy. Many joists overhead had been sawed off by Lieut. Lewis R. Titus of the *Corps D'Afrique*, using a notched table-knife for a saw. In this way the Vermont Yankee obtained pieces for cooking, but he weakened the structure till some officers really feared the roof might come tumbling about our heads; and I remember that the prison commandant, visiting the upper room and gazing heavenward, more than once ejaculated irreverently the name of the opposite region!

Through the kindness of a Confederate officer or bribing the guards a log four or five feet in length is sometimes brought in. Two or three instantly attack it with a blunt piece of iron hoop to start the cleaving, and in less time than one could expect such a work to be done with axes it is split fine with wooden wedges.

Naturally one of the ever-recurring topics of discussion was the glorious dishes we could prepare, if we but had the materials, or of which we would partake if we ever got home again. In our memorandum books we are careful to note down the street and number of the most famous restaurant in each of the largest cities, like Delmonico's in New York or Young's in Boston.

With few exceptions one day is like another. At earliest dawn each of the two floors is covered with about a hundred and seventy-five prostrate forms of officers who have been trying to sleep. Soon some one of them calls in a loud voice. "*Buckets for water!*" The call is repeated. Five or six, who have predetermined to go early to the river Dan that seemed nearly a quarter of a mile distant, start up and seize large wooden pails. They pass to the lower floor. One of them says to the sentinel on duty at the southwest corner door, "Sentry, call the sergeant of the guard; we want to go for water." He complies. In five, ten, or fifteen minutes, a non-commissioned officer, with some half a dozen heavily armed soldiers, comes, the bolts slide, the doors swing, our squad passes out. They are escorted down the hill to the river, and back to prison. By this time it is broad daylight. Many are still lying silent on the floor. Most have risen. Some are washing, or rather wiping with wet handkerchief, face and hands; others are preparing to cook, splitting small blocks of wood for a fire of splinters; a few are nibbling corn bread; here and there one is reading the New Testament. There is no change or adjustment of clothing, for the night dress is the same as the day dress. We no longer wonder how the cured paralytic in Scripture could obey the command, "Take up thy bed and walk"; for at heaviest the bed is but a blanket!

Now, for a half-hour, vengeance on vermin that have plagued us during the night! We daily solve the riddle of the fishermen's answer to "What luck?" the question which puzzled to death

"The blind old bard of Scio's rocky isle,"

"*As many as we caught we left; as many as we could not catch we carry with us*!"

About eight o'clock the cry is heard from the southwest end of the room, "Fall in for roll-call! fall in!" to which several would impudently add, "Here he comes! here he is!" A tall, slim, stooping, beardless, light-haired phenomenon, known as "the roll-call sergeant," enters with two musketeers. We officers having formed in two ranks on the northwest side of the room, he passes down the front from left to right slowly counting. Setting down the number in a memorandum book, he commands in a squeaky feminine voice, "Break ranks," which most of us have already done. Much speculation arose as to the nature and status of this singular being. His face was smooth and childlike, yet dry and wrinkled, so that it was impossible to tell whether he was fifteen or fifty. A committee was said to have waited upon him, and with much apparent deference asked him as to his nativity, his age, and whether he was human or divine, married or single, man or woman. They said he answered sadly, "Alas! I'm no angel, but a married man, thirty-seven years old, from South Carolina. I have three children who resemble me."

Immediately after roll-call, corn bread is brought in for breakfast. It is in large squares about two feet in length and breadth, the top of each square being marked for cutting into twenty or twenty-five rations. Colonel Hooper and Capt. D. Tarbell receive the whole from the rebel commissary, and then distribute to each mess its portion. The mess commissary endeavors to cut it into equal oblong loaves. To make sure of a fair distribution, one officer turns his back, and one after another lays his hand upon a loaf and asks, "Whose is this?" The officer who has faced about names some one as the recipient.

Clear the way now for sweepers. From one end of the room to the other they ply their coarse wooden brooms. Some officers are remarkably neat, and will scrape their floor space with pieces of glass from the broken windows; a few are listless, sullen, utterly despondent, regardless of surroundings, apparently sinking into imbecility; the majority are taking pains to keep up an appearance of respectability.

Many who have been kept awake through the night by cold or rheumatism now huddle around the stoves and try to sleep. Most of the remainder, as the weeks pass, glide into something like a routine of occupations. For several weeks I spent an hour or two every day carving with a broken knife-blade a spoon from a block of hard wood. Sporadic wood-splitting is going on, and cooking appears to be one of the fine arts. An hour daily of oral exercises in French, German, Spanish, Latin, or Italian, under competent teachers, after the Sauveur or Berlitz method, amused and to some extent instructed many. Our cavalry adjutant, Dutch Clark, so called from his skill in the "Pennsylvania Dutch" dialect made perhaps a hundred familiar with the morning salutation, "*Haben Sie gut geschlafen?*" ("Have you slept well?") Lieut. Henry Vander Weyde, A. D.

C., 1st Div., 6th Corps, the artist chum of our principal German instructor, amused many by his pencil portraits of "Slim Jim," the nondescript "roll-call sergeant" of uncertain age and gender; also of some of the sentries, and one or two of his fellow prisoners. A worn-out pack of fifty-two cards, two or three chess and checker boards of our manufacture, and twenty-four rudely carved checker-men and thirty-two fantastic chess-men, furnished frequent amusement to those who understood the games.

On an average once in two days we received about one o'clock what was called soup. We were told, and we believed it to be true, that all the rich nitrogenous portion had been carefully skimmed off for use elsewhere; not thrown away as the fresh maid threw the "scum" that formed on top of the milk!

The topic of most frequent discussion was the prospect of an exchange of prisoners. Our would-be German conversationalists never forgot to ask, "*Haben Sie etwas gehörten von Auswechseln der Gefangenen?*" ("Have you heard anything of exchange of prisoners?") It was hard to believe that our government would leave us to die of starvation.

At the close of the soup hour and after another turn at sweeping, almost every officer again sat down or sat up to rid himself of the *pediculidæ vestimenti*. We called it "skirmishing"; it was rather a pitched battle. The humblest soldier and the brevet major-general must daily strip and fight. Ludicrous, were it not so abominable, was this mortifying necessity. No account of prison life in Danville would be complete without it. Pass by it hereafter in sorrow and silence, as one of those duties which Cicero says are to be done but not talked about.

The occupations of the morning are now largely resumed, but many prefer to lie quiet on the floor for an hour.

An interesting incident that might happen at any time is the arrival in prison of a Confederate newspaper. A commotion near the stairway! Fifty or a hundred cluster around an officer with a clear strong voice, and listen as he reads aloud the news, the editorials, and the selections. The rebels are represented as continually gaining victories, but singularly enough the northern armies are always drawing nearer!

Toward sunset many officers walk briskly half an hour to and fro the length of the room for exercise.

Another roll-call by the mysterious heterogeneous if not hermaphroditical Carolina sergeant!

Brooms again by the mess on duty. Again oral language-lessons by Cook and Putnam. Then discussions or story-telling.

It is growing dark. A candle is lighted making darkness visible. We have many skilful singers, who every evening "discourse most excellent music." They sing *Just before the battle, mother; Do they miss me at home? We shall meet, but we shall miss him* (a song composed on the death of one of my Worcester pupils by Hon. Charles Washburn); *Nearer, My God, to thee,* etc. From the sweet strains of affection or devotion, which suffuse the eyes as we begin to lie down for the night, the music passes to the *Star-spangled Banner, Rally round the flag, John Brown's body lies a'mouldering in the grave,* and the like. Often the "concert" concludes with a comic Dutch song by Captain Cafferty, Co. D, 1st N. Y. Cav.

Sleep begins to seal many eyelids, when someone with a loud voice heard through the whole room starts a series of sharp critical questions, amusing or censorious, thus:

"Who don't skirmish?" This is answered loudly from another quarter.

"Slim Jim." The catechism proceeds, sometimes with two or three distinct responses.

"Who cheats the graveyard?"

"Colonel Sprague."

"Who sketched Fort Darling?"

"Captain Tripp." (He was caught sketching long before, and was refused exchange.)

"Who never washes?"

"Lieutenant Screw-my-upper-jaw-off." (His was an unpronounceable foreign name.)

"Who knows everything?"

"General Duffié." (Duffié was a brave officer, of whom more anon.)

"Who don't know anything?"

"The fools that talk when they should be asleep." (The querists subside at last.)

For warmth we lie in contact with each other "spoon-fashion," in groups of three or more. I had bought a heavy woolen shawl for twenty Confederate dollars, and under it were Captain Cook, Adjutant Clark, and Lieutenant Wilder; I myself wearing my overcoat, and snuggling up to my friend Cook. All four lay as close as possible facing in the same direction. The night wears slowly away. When the floor seemed intolerably hard, one of us would say aloud, "Spoon!" and all four would flop over, and rest on the other side. So we vibrated back and forth from nine o'clock till dawn. We were not comfortable, but in far better circumstances than most of the prisoners. Indeed Captain Cook repeatedly declared he owed his life to our blanket.

CHAPTER VIII

Continual Hope of Exchange of Prisoners—"Flag-of-Truce Fever!"—Attempted Escape by Tunneling—Repeated Escapes by Members of Water Parties, and how we Made the Roll-Call Sergeant's Count Come Out all Right every Time—Plot to Break Out by Violence, and its Tragic End.

OUR principal hope for relief from the increasing privations of prison life and from probable exhaustion, sickness, and death, lay in a possible exchange of prisoners. A belief was prevalent that the patients in hospital would be the first so favored. Hence strenuous efforts were sometimes made to convince the apothecary whom we called doctor, and who often visited us, that a prisoner was ill enough to require removal. Once in the institution, the patients got better food, something like a bed, medical attendance daily, and a more comfortable room. Some of them were shamming, lying in two senses and groaning when the physicians were present, but able to sit up and play euchre the rest of the day and half the night. This peculiar disease, this eagerness to get into hospital or remain there till exchanged by flag of truce, was known as the "flag-of-truce fever" or "flag-of-truce-on-the-brain!"

I recall one striking instance. Lieutenant Gardner, already mentioned, had received six or eight hundred dollars in Confederate currency as the price of a gold watch. But like the prodigal in Scripture he was now in a far country, and had wasted his substance in what he called "righteous" living. And when he had spent all, there arose a mighty famine in that corner of the lower room, and he began to be in want. And he would fain have filled his belly with corn-cob-meal bread, or spoiled black beans, or the little potatoes which the swine didn't eat. And no man gave him enough. And he determined to go to hospital. He gave out that he was desperately sick. I at this time had "quarters" on the floor above. Word was brought to me that my friend was mortally ill, and would thank me to come down and take his last message to his relatives. Alarmed, I instantly went down. I found him with two or three splitting a small log of wood!

"Gardner, I hear you are a little 'under the weather.'"

"Dying, Colonel, dying!"

"What appears to be your disease?"

"Flag-o'-truce-on-the-brain!"

"Ah, you've got the exchange fever?"

"Yes; bad."

"Pulse run high?"

"Three hundred a minute."

"Anything I can do for you?"

"Yes, Colonel, beseech that fool doctor to send me to hospital. Tell him I'm on my last legs. Tell him I only want to die there. Appeal to him in behalf of my poor wife and babies." (Gardner, as I well knew, was a bachelor, and had no children—to speak of.)

"Well, Lieutenant, I'll do anything I properly can for you. Is there anything else?"

"Yes, Colonel; lend me your overcoat to wear to hospital; I'll send it back at once."

"But, Lieutenant, you can't get into the hospital. Your cheeks are too rosy; you're the picture of health."

"I'm glad you mentioned that, Colonel. I'll fix that. You'll see."

Next morning he watched at the window, and when he saw the doctor coming, he swallowed a large pill of plug tobacco. The effect was more serious than he expected. In a few minutes he became sick in earnest, and was frightened. A deathlike pallor supervened. When the doctor reached him, there was a genuine fit of vomiting. The story runs that Captain Tiemann made a pathetic appeal in behalf of the imaginary twin babies, that the doctor diagnosed it as a clear case of puerperal (which he pronounced "puerpērial") fever complicated with symptoms of cholera infantum, and ordered him to hospital at once! I loaned the patient my overcoat, which he sent back directly. His recovery seemed miraculous. In a week or two he returned from his delightful outing. This was in the latter part of November.

Previously, for some weeks, Captain Howe and three or four other strong and determined officers managed to get into the cellar of a one-story building contiguous to ours and thence to excavate a tunnel out beyond the line on which the sentinels were perpetually pacing to and fro. I was too feeble to join in the enterprise, but hoped to improve the opportunity to escape when the work was done. Unfortunately the arching top of the tunnel was too near the surface of the ground, and the thin crust gave way under the weight of a sentry. He yelled "Murder!" Two or three of our diggers came scurrying back. The guard next to him shouted, "You Yanks! you G—d d—d Yanks!" and fired into the deep hole. No more tunneling at Danville. [8]

More successful and more amusing were several attempts by individual officers one at a time. The water parties of four to eight went under a strong guard two or three times a day down a long hill to the river Dan. On the slope alongside the path were a number of large brick ovens,[9] in which, we were told, the Confederates used to bake those big squares of corn bread. The iron doors when we passed were usually open. On the way back from the river, one officer on some pretense or other would lag behind the rearmost soldier of the guard, who would turn to hurry him up. The next officer, as soon as the soldier's back was turned, would dodge into an open oven, and the careless guards now engaged in a loud and passionate controversy about slavery or secession would not miss him! Then, as night came on, the negroes in the vicinity, who, like all the rest of the colored people, were friendly to us, would supply the escaped officer with food and clothing, and pilot him on his way rejoicing toward the Union lines. One by one, six officers escaped in that way, and many of us began to look forward to the time when our turn would come to try the baking virtues of those ovens!

But it was important that the escaped officer should not be missed. How should we deceive the nondescript that we called "the roll-call sergeant"? Morning and evening he carefully counted every one. How make the census tally with the former enumerations? Yankee ingenuity was here put to a severe test; but Lieutenant Titus, before mentioned, solved the problem. With his table-knife saw he cut a hole about two feet square in the floor near the northeast corner of the upper room. A nicely fitting trapdoor completed the arrangement. Through this hole, helped by a rude rope ladder of strips of rags, and hoisted to the shoulders of a tall man by strong arms from below, a nimble officer could quickly ascend. Now those in the lower room were counted first. When they broke ranks, and the human automaton faced to the west and moved slowly towards the stairs with three or four "Yanks" clustering at his side in earnest conversation, the requisite number of spry young prisoners would "shin up" the ladder, emerge, "deploy," and be counted over again in the upper room! The thing worked to a charm. Not one of the six was missed.

Unfortunately, however, two or three of them were recaptured and again incarcerated in Libby. The Richmond authorities thereupon telegraphed to Colonel Smith, asking how those officers escaped from Danville. Smith, surprised, ordered a recount. The trapdoor did its duty. "All present!" Finally he answered, "No prisoner has escaped from Danville." The rebel commissary of prisons at Richmond, Gen. J. H. Winder, then telegraphed the names of the recaptured officers. Smith looks on his books: there are those names, sure enough! The mystery must be solved. He now sends his adjutant to count us about noon. We asked him what it meant. He told us it was reported that several officers had escaped. We replied, "That's too good to be true." He counted very slowly and with extraordinary precision. He kept his eye on the staircase as he approached it. Six officers flew up the ladder as we huddled around him. It was almost impossible to suppress laughter at the close, when he declared, "I'll take my oath no prisoner has escaped from this prison." But there were those names of the missing, and there was our ill-disguised mirth. Smith resorted to heroic measures. He came in with two or three of his staff and a man who was said to be a professor of mathematics. This was on the 8th of November, 1864. He made all officers of the lower room move for a half-hour into the upper room, and there fall in line with the rest. His adjutant called the roll in reality. Each as his name was read aloud was made to step forward and cross to the other side. Of course no one could answer for the absent six. I doubt if he ever learned the secret of that trapdoor. The professor of mathematics promised to bring me a Geometry. About two weeks later, November 24th, he brought me a copy of Davies's *Legendre*.

On the 9th of December, while our senior officer, General Hayes, was sick in hospital, the next in rank, Gen. A. N. Duffié, of the First Cavalry Division of Sheridan's army, fresh from the French service, with which he had campaigned in Algeria, where he was wounded nine times, suddenly conceived a plot to break out and escape. Two companies of infantry had arrived in the forenoon and stacked their arms in plain sight on the level ground about twenty rods distant. Duffié's plan was to rush through the large open door when a water party returning with filled buckets should be entering, seize those muskets, overpower the guard, immediately liberate the thousand or fifteen hundred Union prisoners in the three other Danville prisons, and push off to our lines in East Tennessee. He had Sheridan's *élan*, not Grant's cool-headed strategy. With proper preparation and organization, such as Hayes would have insisted upon, it might have been a success. He called us, field officers about twenty, together and laid the matter before us. No vote was taken, but I think a majority were opposed to the whole scheme. He was disposed to consider himself, though a prisoner, as still vested with authority to command all of lower rank, and he expected them to obey him without question. In this view many acquiesced, but others dissented. By his request, though doubtful of his right to command and in feeble health, I drew up a pledge for those to sign who were willing to engage in the projected rising and would promise to obey. It was found that at least one hundred and fifty could be counted on. Colonel Ralston, previously mentioned, was the chief opponent of the outbreak, but he recognized Duffié's authority and insisted upon our submission to it. Similar appeared to be the attitude of the following colonels:

Gilbert H. Prey, 104th N. Y.

James Carle, 191st Pa.

T. B. Kaufman, 209th Pa.

W. Ross Hartshorne, 190th Pa.

Of the lieutenant-colonels, most of the following doubted the success, but would do their best to promote it, if commanded:

Charles H. Tay, 10th N. J.

Theodore Gregg, 45th Pa.

G. A. Moffett, 94th N. Y.

J. S. Warner, 121st Pa.

George Hamett, 147th N. Y.

Charles H. Hooper, 24th Mass.

Homer B. Sprague, 13th Conn.

So the following majors: A. W. Wakefield, 49th Pa.; G. S. Horton, 58th Mass.; E. F. Cooke, 2d N. Y. Cav.; John G. Wright, 51st N. Y.; J. V. Peale, 4th Pa. Cav.; John W. Byron, 88th N. Y.; David Sadler, 2d Pa. Heavy Art.; John Byrne, 155th N. Y.; E. O. Shepard, 32d Mass.; J. A. Sonders, 8th Ohio Cav.; Charles P. Mattocks, 17th Maine; E. S. Moore, Paymaster; Wm. H. Fry, 16th Pa. Cav.; Milton Wendler, 191st Pa.; James E. Deakins, 8th Tenn. Cav.; Geo. Haven Putnam, Adjt. and later Bvt.-Major, 176th N. Y.

All of the foregoing then present and not on the sick list should have been most thoroughly instructed as to their duties, and should have been enabled to communicate all needed information to the forty-six captains and one hundred and thirty-three lieutenants, who, though many were sadly reduced in vitality, were accounted fit for active service. I had repeatedly noticed in battle the perplexity of company, regimental, or even brigade commanders, from lack of information as to the necessary movements in unforeseen emergencies. It is not enough to say, as one corps commander (Hancock?) is said to have done during the Battle of the Wilderness in May, 1864, to a newly arrived colonel with his regiment, who inquired, "Where shall I go in?" "Oh, anywhere; there's lovely fighting all along the line!"

Here the step most vital to success, the *sine qua non*, was to keep that outside door open for the outrush of two hundred men. To this end, eight of our strongest and most determined, under a dashing leader like Colonel Hartshorne or Lieutenant-Colonel Gregg, should have been sent out as a water party. Instead, Captain Cook, who was brave enough, but then physically weak, hardly able to carry a pail of water, was the leader of an average small squad, "the spirit indeed willing, but the flesh weak."

Hardly less important was it to select a dozen or twenty of the most fierce and energetic, to be at the head of the stairs in perfect readiness to dash instantly through the opening door and assist the water party in disarming their guards, and, without a moment's pause, followed by the whole two hundred, pounce upon the guard house. Ralston or Duffié himself should have headed this band. Simultaneously, without a second's interval, three or four desperate, fiery, powerful officers, detailed for the purpose, should have grappled with the sentinel on duty in the middle of the lower room and disarmed and gagged him.

Besides the field officers, we had with us many subordinates of great intelligence like Capt. Henry S. Burrage of the 36th Mass., Lieut. W. C. B. Goff of the 1st D. C. Cav., Lieut. W. C. Howe, 2d Mass. Cav., Adjt. James A. Clark, 17th Pa. Cav., and the artist, Lieut. Henry Vander Weyde; and nothing would have been easier than for Duffié to communicate through them to every officer the most complete and precise information and instructions.

Scarcely any of these precautions were taken. The general was impatient. The next day, December 10th, he issued his command in these words: "I order the attempt to be made, and I call upon all of you, who have not forgotten how to obey orders, to follow." The water party was immediately sent out, and its return was watched for. He and Ralston, without the help of a third, made the mistake of personally grappling with the floor sentry, a brave, strong, red-headed fellow, and they tackled him a moment too soon. He stoutly resisted. They wrested his musket from him. He yelled. They tried to stop his mouth. Instantly the door began to swing open a little. The water party, too few and too weak, paralyzed, failed to act. The foremost of us sprang from the stairs to the door. Before we could reach it, it was slammed to, bolted and barred against us! With several others I rushed to the windows and tried to tear off the heavy bars. In vain. The soldiers outside began firing through the broken panes. Ralston was shot through the body. We assisted him up the stairs while the bullets were flying. In less than five minutes from the moment when he and Duffié seized the sentinel, it was all over. In about a quarter of an hour, Colonel

Smith came in with his adjutant and two or three guards, and ordered Ralston removed to hospital. As he was carried out, one of us expressed the hope that the wound was not serious. He answered in the language of Mercutio, "No, 'tis not so deep as a well, nor so wide as a church door; but 'tis enough, 'twill serve." He knew it was mortal, and expressed a willingness to die for his country in the line of duty. He passed away next morning. Colonel Smith expressed sorrow for him, and surprise at the ingratitude of us who had been guilty of insurrection against his gentle sway!

A strict search for possible weapons followed during which we were told we must give up our United States money. I saved a ten-dollar greenback by concealing it in my mouth "as an ape doth nuts in the corner of his jaw," all the while munching corn bread, gnawing two holes in the bill!

FOOTNOTES:

[8] "You will doubtless recall the man-hole worked through the heavy brick wall, made during the 'stilly nights,' opening into the attic of an annex to the main building. We found our way down by means of a rope ladder, and started our tunnel under the basement floor. But for the exposure we would have emptied the prison. To find the way down we gave them a lively hunt!—And those *epithets*!—I have a blouse with a rent in the back made in going through that hole in the wall."—Howe's *Letter* of Jan. 30, 1914.

For further particulars of this attempt to tunnel out, see Major Putnam's *A Prisoner of War in Virginia*, pp. 55-60.

[9] Putnam describes them as disused furnaces. They may have been both.

CHAPTER IX

Kind Clergymen Visit us and Preach Excellent Discourses—Colonel Smith's Personal Good Will to me—His Offer—John F. Ficklin's Charity—My Good Fortune—Supplies of Clothing Distributed—Deaths in Prison.

Union men never looked upon Confederates as mortal enemies. Whenever a flag of truce was flying, both were disposed to shake hands and exchange favors. I recollect that our Captain Burrage complained that he was unfairly captured when he was engaged in a friendly deal with a Confederate between the lines. At Port Hudson, when the white signal was to go down, we gave the "Johnnies" fair warning, shouting, "RATS! TO YOUR HOLES!" before we fired on them. But war cannot be conducted on peace principles, and in a flash a man acts like a devil. In an open window near the spot where I slept, an officer upset a cup of water, and a few drops fell on the head of the guard outside. Instantly he fired. The bullet missed, passed through the window below and the floor above, and lodged in the hand or arm of another officer. I had an opportunity to express to Colonel Smith my angry disgust at such savagery. He agreed that the fellow ought to be punished—"at least for not being able to shoot straighter!"[10]

Kindly visits were sometimes paid us. Two young men from the Richmond Young Men's Christian Association came. The wicked said, "One came 'to pray with us all right,' the other 'to prey upon us all wrong'"; for the latter tried to induce us to exchange greenbacks for rebel currency!

Several times we were visited by kind clergymen who preached excellent sermons. The first was Rev. —— Dame of Danville. He was, I think, an Episcopal minister. He was a high Mason, a gentleman of very striking appearance, with a beautiful flowing beard, that would have done honor to Moses or Aaron. As we sat on the hard floor, two hundred listening reverently to his choice language, he seemed to foresee the doom which many of us had begun to fear, and he very appropriately and with much earnestness bade us consider our latter end. Mentioning his name with gratitude some thirty years afterwards in a lecture at the Mountain

Lake Chautauqua, Md., one of my audience gave me a photograph of the minister's handsome face, and told me he was greatly beloved. I doubt not he deserved it.

Rev. Charles K. Hall of Danville, a Methodist Episcopal clergyman, came to us a little later. His first sermon was an eloquent discourse on Charity. He practiced what he preached; for he never came empty-handed. On his first visit he brought armfuls of tobacco, each plug wrapped in a pious tract. He asked us to fall in line, for he had something for each. When he came to me in the distribution, I declined it, saying "I never use tobacco in any form." "Oh take it," said he; "you read the tract, and give the tobacco to your neighbor." On subsequent Sundays he brought eggs and other delicacies for the sick. We admired him as a preacher, and regarded him with affection as a man. Secession and slavery aside, for he believed in the rightfulness of both, as we learned on arguing with him, it would be hard to find a more lovable character than Charles K. Hall. And the South was full of such, who would have been glad, if permitted and opportunity offered, to be good Samaritans, neighbors to him who had fallen among foes; pure, gentle, kindly spirits, to whom it will be said in the last great day, "I was an hungred and ye gave me meat; I was sick, and ye visited me; I was in prison, and ye came unto me."

From the lack of sufficient and proper food, clothing, and exercise, the health of all suffered. Much of the time it was impossible to keep warm. The most prevalent diseases, I think, were rheumatism and scurvy. I suffered from both. Anti-scorbutics were scarce. The pain from rheumatism was slight during the day; but at evening it began in the joints of the fingers and became more severe as night advanced, ascending from the hands to the wrists, arms, and shoulders. It was worst at midnight and through the small hours, then gradually diminished till daylight. The prison physician did his best to help us with liniment, but in those winter nights the treatment was ineffective.

Upon the total failure of our attempt to break out on the 10th of December, and having come reluctantly to the conclusion that Colonel Smith had told us the truth when he said that Lincoln and Grant would not consent to an exchange of prisoners, I foresaw that death was inevitable after a few months, perhaps a few weeks, unless the situation should materially change for the better. I determined, though without much hope of success, to appeal to Colonel Smith for personal favor. On the 15th of December I sent word to him that I wished an interview with him. He immediately sent a soldier to bring me to his office. He received me courteously; for he was a gentleman. I told him it was necessary for me, if I was to live much longer, that I should at least have better food and more of it. I asked him if it would not be possible for an arrangement to be effected whereby some of my relatives in the north should furnish a Confederate prisoner with food, clothing, and comforts, and that prisoner's relatives in the south should reciprocate by supplying me. He answered that it might be possible, but he did not know of any such southern captive's friends likely to respond. After a few minutes of silence he said:

"Colonel Sprague, I'd like to do something for you, and I'll make you an offer."

"Well?"

"Your government has adopted the devilish policy of no exchange of prisoners."

"I am afraid it's true."

"I know it's true."

"Well, what's your proposition?"

"I am overworked here. I must do my duty to my government. Our cause is just."

"Well?"

"I should like to have you assist me by doing writing regularly for me at these headquarters. I would parole you. You shall have a room to yourself, a good bed, plenty of food, and a good deal of liberty. You must give me your word of honor not to attempt to escape."

"Colonel Smith, I thank you. I appreciate the friendly spirit in which you make the offer, and I am very grateful for it. But I can't conscientiously accept it. I am in the Union Army, bound to do everything in my power to destroy your government. I must do nothing to help it. If Lincoln refuses to exchange us prisoners, it may be best for the United States, though hard on us. What happens to us is a minor matter. It's a soldier's business to die for his country rather than help its enemies in the slightest degree. I can't entertain your proposal."

So the conference ended sadly. As I was leaving his office he introduced me to a Confederate soldier who sat there and who had heard the whole conversation. Next day this soldier entered the prison by permission of Colonel Smith and brought me some nice wheat bread, some milk, pickles, and other food, a pair of thick woolen stockings, and a hundred dollars in Confederate money. He gave me his name, John F. Ficklin, of the Virginia *Black Horse Cavalry*. He whispered to me that he was at heart a Union man, but had been forced by circumstances to enter the Confederate service; that by simulating illness he had got relieved from duty at the front and assigned to service at Colonel Smith's headquarters; that he was confident he could bring about such an arrangement for reciprocal supplies as I had proposed, and had so informed Smith, who approved of the plan; that until such a plan should be put in operation he would furnish me from his own table. He said to me very privately that he was greatly moved by what I had said the day before. "But," he added, "I am not entirely unselfish in this. I foresee that the Confederacy can't last very long; certainly not a year. I give it till next September; and, frankly, when it goes to smash, I want to stand well with you officers." At my suggestion he gave a few other prisoners food and money.

In a few days I was again called to headquarters to meet a Mr. Jordan, who, through Ficklin's efforts, had been invited to meet me. His son, Henry T. Jordan, Adjutant of the 55th North Carolina Regiment, was at that time a prisoner at Johnson's Island, Ohio. Mr. Jordan agreed to make out a list of articles which he wished my relatives to send to his son. In a day or two he did so. I likewise made out a statement of my immediate wants, as follows:

Wood for cooking;
Cup, plate, knife, fork, spoon;
Turnips, salt, pepper, rice, vinegar;
Pickled cucumbers, dried apple, molasses;
Or any other substantial food.

I asked Jordan to send me those things *at once*. He answered after some delay that he would do so immediately on receiving an acknowledgment from his son that my friends had furnished him what he wanted; and he would await such a message! As my relatives were in Massachusetts and Connecticut, it would take considerable time for them to negotiate with the prison commandant and other parties in Ohio and have the stipulations distinctly understood and carried into effect there. Besides, there were likely to be provoking delays in communicating by mail between the north and the south, and it might be a month or six weeks before he got assurances from his son; by which time I should probably be in a better world than Danville, and in no need of wood, food, or table-ware. I wrote him to that effect, and requested him to make haste, but received no reply.

My friend Mr. Ficklin came to the rescue. As a pretext to deceive, if need were, the prison authorities, and furnish to them and others a sufficient reason for bringing me supplies, he pretended that he had a friend, a Confederate prisoner of war at Camp Douglas near Chicago, and that Colonel Sprague's friends had been exceedingly kind to him, ministering most liberally to his wants! The name of this imaginary friend was J. H. Holland, a private soldier of the 30th Virginia Cavalry. Ficklin forged a letter purporting to come from Holland to him, which he showed to Colonel Smith, in which he spoke with much gratitude of my friends' bounty, and besought Ficklin to look tenderly after my comfort in return! The ruse succeeded. Ficklin's generosity to me was repeated from time to time, and perhaps saved my life.

A year after the close of the war Ficklin wrote to me that he wished to secure a position in the Treasury Department of the United States, and he thought it would aid him if I would certify to what I knew of his kindness to Union prisoners. I accordingly drew up a strong detailed statement of his timely and invaluable charities to us in our distress. I accompanied it with vouchers for my credibility signed by Hon. N. D. Sperry, General Wm. H. Russell, and President Theodore D. Woolsey, all of New Haven, and Governor Wm. A. Buckingham of Norwich, Conn. These documents I forwarded to Ficklin. I do not know the result.

From Sergeant Wilson F. Smith, chief clerk at Colonel Smith's headquarters, a paroled prisoner, member of Co. F., 6th Pa. Cav., the company of Captain Furness, son or brother of my Shakespearian friend, Dr. Horace Howard Furness, and from Mr. Strickland, undertaker, who furnished the coffins and buried the dead of the Danville prisons, both of whom I talked with when I was on parole in February, '65, I obtained statistics mutually corroborative of the number of deaths in the Danville prisons. In November there were 130; in December, 140; from January 1st to January 24th, 105. The negro soldiers suffered most. There were sixty-four of them living in prison when we reached Danville, October 20, '64. Fifty-seven of them were dead on the 12th of February, '65, when I saw and talked with the seven survivors in Prison No. Six. From one of the officers (I think it was Captain Stuart) paroled like myself in February to distribute supplies of clothing sent by the United States through the lines, and who performed that duty in Salisbury, and from soldiers of my own regiment there imprisoned, I learned that in the hundred days ending February 1st, out of eight or ten thousand prisoners, more than thirty a day, more than three thousand in all, had died! Of Colonel Hartshorne's splendid "Bucktail Regiment," the 190th Pa., formerly commanded by my Yale classmate Colonel O'Neil who fell at Antietam, there were 330 at Salisbury, October 19th, the day we left; 116 of them were dead before February 1st, one company losing 22 out of 33 men.

Why this fearful mortality? Men do not die by scores, hundreds, thousands, without some extraordinary cause. It was partly for want of clothing. They were thinly clad when captured.

Pursuant to agreement entered into early in December, 1864, between the Federal and Confederate authorities, supplies of clothing for Union prisoners in Richmond, Danville, and Salisbury, were sent through the lines. They did not reach Danville till February. Colonel Carle, 191st Pa. and myself, with another officer (I think he was Colonel Gilbert G. Prey, 104th N. Y.) were paroled to distribute coats (or blouses), trousers, and shoes, among the enlisted men in their three prisons. Then for the first time Union officers saw the interior of those jails. By permission of Colonel Smith, Mr. Ficklin accompanied us on one of these visits, and I saw him give fifty dollars in Confederate money to one of our suffering soldiers. My part in the distribution was to sign as witness opposite the name of each one receiving. Those rolls should be in the archives at Washington.

On the 12th of February we issued shoes and clothing in the jail known as Prison No. Six. It contained that day 308 of our men. There were the seven surviving colored soldiers, and the one wearing our prison commander's coat. We requested them all to form line, and each as his name was called to come forward and receive what he most needed. Some of them were so feeble that they had to be assisted in coming down from the upper floor, almost carried in the arms of stronger comrades. Many were unable to remain standing long, and sank helpless on the floor. Nearly all were half-clad, or wearing only the thinnest of garments. Some were white with vermin. Several were so far gone that they had forgotten their company or regiment. Every one seemed emaciated. Many kept asking me why our government did not exchange prisoners; for they were told every day the truth that the Confederate government desired it. There was a stove, but no fuel. The big rooms were not heated. The cold was severe. About a third of them had apparently given up all hope of keeping their limbs and bodies warm; but they kept their heads, necks, shoulders, and chests, carefully wrapped. The dismal coughing at times drowned all other sounds, and made it difficult to proceed with our work of distribution. There were two little fires of chips and splinters on bricks, one of them near the middle, the other near the far end. In contact with these were tin or earthen cups containing what passed for food or drink. There was no outlet for smoke. It blackened the hands and faces of those nearest, and irritated the lungs of all.

This prison was the worst. It was colder than the others. But all were uncomfortably cold. All were filled with smoke and lice. From each there went every day to the hospital a wagon-load of half-starved and broken-hearted soldiers who would never return. I visited the hospital to deliver to two of the patients letters which Colonel Smith had handed to me for them. They were both dead. I looked down the long list. The word "Died," with the date, was opposite most of the names. As I left the hospital I involuntarily glanced up at the lintel, half expecting to see inscribed there as over the gate to Dante's Hell,

ALL HOPE ABANDON, YE WHO ENTER HERE!

At the rate our enlisted men were dying at Danville and Salisbury during the winter of 1864-65, all would have passed away in a few months, certainly in less than a year; AND THEY KNEW IT.

Is it any wonder that some of them, believing our government had abandoned them to starvation rather than again risk its popularity by resorting to conscription for the enrollment of recruits and by possibly stirring up draft riots such as had cost more than a thousand lives in the city of New York in July, 1863, accepted at last the terms which the Confederates constantly held out to them, took the oath of allegiance to the Confederacy, and enlisted in the rebel army? I was credibly informed that more than forty did it in Prison No. Four at Danville, and more than eleven hundred at Salisbury. Confederate recruiting officers and sergeants were busy in those prisons, offering them the choice between death and life. No doubt multitudes so enlisted under the Confederate flag with full determination to desert to our lines at the first convenient opportunity. Such was the case with private J. J. Lloyd, Co. A, of my battalion, who rejoined us in North Carolina. *The great majority chose to die.*

The last communication that I received from enlisted men of my battalion, fellow prisoners with me at Salisbury, whom I had exhorted not to accept the offers of the Confederates, but to be true to their country and their flag, read thus: "Colonel, don't be discouraged. Our boys all say they'll starve to death in prison sooner than take the oath of allegiance to the Confederacy." And true to this resolve did indeed starve or freeze to death Sergeant Welch, Sergeant Twichell, Privates Vogel, Plaum, Barnes, Geise, Andrews, Bishop, Weldon, who had stood by me in many a battle, and who died at last for the cause they loved.

It is comparatively easy to face death in battle. No great courage or merit in that. The soldier is swept along with the mass. Often he cannot shirk if he would. The chances usually are that he will come out alive. He may be inspired with heroism,

> And the stern joy which warriors feel
> In foeman worthy of their steel.

There is a consciousness of irresistible strength as he beholds the gleaming lines, the dense columns, the smoking batteries, the dancing flags, the cavalry with flying feet.

> 'Twere worth ten years of peaceful life,

One glance at their array.

Or nobler, he feels that he represents a nation or a grand cause, and that upon his arm depends victory. In his enthusiasm he even fancies himself a vicegerent of the Almighty, commissioned to fight in His cause, to work His will, to save His earth from becoming a hell. "From the heights of yonder pyramids," said Napoleon to the French battling against the Mamelukes, "forty centuries are looking down upon you." Our soldier in battle imagined the world looking on, that for him there was fame undying; should he fall wounded, his comrades would gently care for him; if slain, his country's flag would be his shroud.

By no such considerations were our imprisoned comrades cheered. Not in the glorious rush and shock of battle; not in hope of victory or fadeless laurels; no angel charities, or parting kiss, or sympathetic voice bidding the soul look heavenward while the eye was growing dim; no dear star-spangled banner for a winding sheet. But wrapped in rags; unseen, unnoticed, dying by inches, in the cold, in the darkness, often in rain or sleet, houseless, homeless, friendless, on the hard floor or the bare ground, starving, freezing, broken-hearted.

O the long and dreary winter!
O the cold and cruel winter!

It swept them away at Salisbury by tens, twenties, even fifties in a single night.

These men preferred death to dishonor. When we are told that our people are not patriotic, or sigh of America as Burke did of France a century and a quarter ago, that the age of chivalry is gone, we may point to this great martyrdom, the brightest painting on the darkest background in all our history—thousands choosing to die for the country which seemed to disown them!

My diary records, and I believe it correct, that on the 17th of February, there were ten deaths in the Danville prisons. A little before midnight of that day the Danville prisoners were loaded into box cars, and the train was started for Richmond. Three, it was reported, died in the cars that night, and one next morning in the street on the way to Libby.

During the next three days I obtained the autographs of two hundred and fifteen of my fellow officers there. The little book is precious. A few still survive; but the great majority have joined the faithful whom they commanded.

On Fame's eternal camping ground
    Their silent tents are spread,
And Glory guards with solemn round
    The bivouac of the dead!

On the twenty-second we were taken for exchange down the James. As we passed through the lines into what we were accustomed fondly to call "God's Country," salvos of artillery and signs of universal rejoicing greeted us. Our reception made us imagine for an hour that our arrival perceptibly heightened the general joy of the Washington anniversary. But many of us could not help wishing we were asleep with the thousands who were filling nameless graves at Danville and Salisbury.

FOOTNOTES:

[10] See Putnam's account of this incident in his *A Prisoner of War in Virginia*, p. 67.

CHAPTER X

Results and Reflections—The Right and the Wrong of it All.

A FEW days of waiting in the buildings of the Naval Academy at Annapolis while exchange papers were preparing gave us opportunity for a much-needed transformation. Our old clothing, encrusted with dirt and infested with vermin, in many cases had to be destroyed. One of our number especially unkempt, Captain T., who gave up for an hour or two his beloved trousers, found to his surprise and horror when he called for their return that they had been burned with four hundred dollars in greenbacks sewed up in the lining! We smiled at his irrepressible grief; it was poetic justice. He had carefully concealed the fact of his being flush, pretending all along to be like the rest *in forma pauperis*, and contriving, it was said, to transfer in crooked ways our pennies into his pockets!

Fumigated, parboiled, scrubbed, barbered, decently clothed, "the deformed transformed" were once more presentable in civilized society. Then followed a brief leave of absence if desired, to visit relatives. To them it seemed a veritable resurrection after our months of living burial; yet the joy of reunion was sometimes tinged with sorrow. I learned that in the very week in which the tidings of my capture came our home circle had been sadly broken by the death of a beloved sister, and just then the telegraph told of the loss by fever in the army at Newbern of our household darling,

> Younger by fifteen years than myself,
> Brother at once and son.

As previously stated we who held commissions fared better on the whole than the non-commissioned officers and privates, though receiving from the commissary rations exactly equal to theirs. Commonly older and therefore of larger experience and superior intelligence, a good officer is as a father looking out for the physical welfare of his men as well as himself. Then there were some who, like Gardner, had been fortunate in keeping clothing, money, or other valuable at the instant of capture or in hiding it when searched by Dick Turpin at Libby. Several like Captain Cook had obtained pecuniary assistance from influential friends across the lines, or in a few instances had been favored by brother freemasons or by charitably disposed visitors who gave us a little food, a few old books, or even Confederate currency. Several sold to the sentinels watches, rings, chains, breast-pins, society badges, silver spurs, military boots, or curiously wrought specimens of Yankee ingenuity carved with infinite pains. The "Johnnies" appeared to hanker for any article not produced in the Confederacy. An officer of the guard offered Putnam three hundred dollars for a nearly worn-out tooth-brush!

The educational standard among our officers was quite respectable. I think that West Point had a representative among us, as well as Bowdoin and several other colleges. Certainly we had ex-students from at least five universities, Brown, Yale, Harvard, the Sorbonne, and Göttingen.

To afford diversion and as an antidote to depression, as well as for intellectual improvement, some of us studied mathematics[11] or *Shakespeare*. Three or four classes were formed in modern languages. We had card-playing with packs soiled and worn; checkers and chess on extemporized boards with rudely whittled "pieces"; occasional discussions historical, literary, political, or religious; many of us quite regular physical exercises in brisk walks on the empty lowest floor; story-telling; at times, though not often, the reading aloud of a Confederate newspaper, to a group of fifty or more listeners; at evening, sweet singing, riddles, jests, or loud-voiced sarcastic conundrums and satirical responses. Many found interest and pleasure in carving with the utmost nicety wood or bone.[12]

Something like military discipline prevailed among the two hundred in the upper room where the superior rank of General Hayes was often recognized. Among a hundred and fifty or more in the lower room, where for a month or two I was the senior but was unwilling to assume precedence, I secured with the aid of Major Byron, Captain Howe, and a few others a sort of civil government with semi-military features.

These measures and the favoring circumstances that have been mentioned tended of course to the preservation of health among the officers. There was severe suffering from hunger, cold, rheumatism, and scurvy, from all of which I was for weeks a victim and at one time seemed doomed to perish. I recall, however, the names of but two officers (there were said to be four) who died at Danville. Some of us, though enfeebled, were soon able to rejoin our commands; as Putnam his at Newbern in April, Gardner and I ours at Morehead City the day after Lee's surrender at Appomattox.

Of the effect in after-life of these strange experiences it is safe to say that to some extent they were a spur to intellectual effort. At least they should have made all sadder and wiser; and they certainly were in some cases an equipment for descriptive authorship. Major (Adner A.) Small wrote a valuable account of prison life. Dr. Burrage's narratives of his capture and its results are entertaining and instructive. Major Putnam's *A Prisoner of War in Virginia* (reprinted in his *Memories of My Youth*) is an important contribution to our military history.[13] Lieutenant Estabrooks's *Adrift in Dixie* is charmingly told.[14] "Dutch Clark" (Adjutant James A. Clark, 17th Pa. Cav.), one of the four who nightly tried to sleep under my blanket, started and edited with ability at Scranton *The Public Code*, for which I was glad to furnish literary material. He afterwards became prominent in theosophic circles. Others distinguished themselves. Captain (Frank H.) Mason, in prison our best chess player, was long Consul-General at Paris. Cook studied five or six years in Germany, France, and Italy, then was for eight or ten years assistant professor in German at Harvard, and afterwards for two years, until his untimely death, professor in the same department at the Institute of Technology in Boston. In addressing a Sunday-school in Brooklyn, 1871, I unexpectedly lighted upon Captain Tiemann doing good work as a teacher. Captain Gardner continued for many months a model military officer in Georgia.[15] I remained in the service a full year, often on courts-martial, military commissions, and "reconstruction" duty.

As already described, the condition of the enlisted men strongly contrasted with ours. The Report of the Confederate Inspector of Prisons now on file in the *War Records* of our government, though the reports of his subordinate officers are significantly missing, covers the few months next preceding January, 1865. It sharply censures the immediate prison authorities, stating, as the result of the privations, that the deaths at Danville were at the rate of about five per day! I think they were more numerous in

January and February. None of my battalion were there, but at Salisbury three-sevenths of them died in less than three months!

It is hard to refrain from the expression of passionate indignation at the treatment accorded to our non-commissioned officers and privates in those southern hells. For years we were accustomed to ask, "In what military prison of the north, in what common jail of Europe, in what dungeon of the civilized or savage world, have captives taken in war—nay, condemned criminals—been systematically exposed to a lingering death by cold and hunger? The foulest felon—his soul black with sacrilege, his hands reeking with parricide—has enough of food, of clothing, of shelter; a chair to sit in, a fire to warm him, a blanket to hide his nakedness, a bed of straw to die on!"

But listen a moment to the other side. Alexander H. Stephens, Vice-President of the Confederacy, afterwards for eight years a representative in our Congress, a man of unquestioned integrity, shows in his *War between the States* (pub. 1868-70) by quotation from the Report of our then Secretary of War (July 19, 1866) that only 22,576 Federal prisoners died in Confederate hands during the war, whilst 26,436 Confederate prisoners died in Federal hands. He shows also from the United States Surgeon-General Joseph K. Barnes's Report that the number of Federal prisoners in southern prisons was about 270,000, but the number of Confederate prisoners in northern prisons was about 220,000; so that the percentage of deaths in southern prisons was under nine, while the percentage of deaths in northern prisons was over twelve![16]

Had there been, from the first, prompt exchanges of prisoners between the north and the south, few of these forty-nine thousand lives would have been lost. *Who, then, blocked the exchange?*

Stephens declares (*War between the States*, vol. ii):

> "It is now well understood to have been a part of the settled policy of the Washington authorities in conducting the war, not to exchange prisoners. The grounds upon which this extraordinary course was adopted were, that it was humanity to the northern men in the field to let their captured comrades perish in prison rather than to let an

equal number of Confederate soldiers be released on exchange to meet them in battle."

To the same effect our Secretary Stanton in one of his letters in 1864 pointed out "that it would not be good policy to send back to be placed on the firing line 70,000 able-bodied Confederates, and to receive in exchange men who, with but few exceptions, were not strong enough to hold their muskets."

The responsibility, then, for this refusal and the consequent enormous sacrifice of life with all the accompanying miseries, must rest in part upon the Government of the United States.[17]

Blame not the tender-hearted Lincoln for this.

Did he not judge wisely? Was it not best for the nation that we prisoners should starve and freeze?

The pivotal question for him and Grant and Stanton was, "Shall we exchange and thereby enable the South to reinforce their armies with fifty to a hundred thousand trained soldiers?

"If yes, then we must draft many more than that; for they being on the defensive we must outnumber them in battle. If no, then we must either stop their cruelties by equally cruel retaliation, as Washington hung André for the execution of Hale, or we must, more cruelly still, leave myriads of our soldiers to sink into imbecility and death."

The North had not the excuse of destitution which the South had, and it could not bring itself to make reprisals in kind. To draft again, as evinced in the terrible riots of July, 1863, would have been extremely unpopular and perhaps overthrown the administration and defeated the policy of the government. To exchange would pretty surely have prolonged the war, and might have resulted in permanent disunion.

As to the right or wrong of the refusal to exchange, it is hardly relevant to insist that the triumph of the South would have perpetuated slavery. Lincoln's Proclamation, January 1, 1863, did not touch slavery in the Border States. And from the southern nation, denuded of slaves by their escape to the North and confronted by the growing anti-slavery sentiment of the civilized world, the "peculiar institution" would soon have died out.

Need we attempt, as is often done, to justify our government's attitude in this matter by affirming that the nation was in a life-and-death struggle for its very existence? Did that existence depend upon its territorial limits? Would it have gone to pieces if the victorious North had relinquished its hold on the defeated South? Had a boundary line been drawn half-way across the continent, separating the twenty-three loyal States from the eleven seceding, the twenty-two millions of the North from the nine or ten millions of the South, would it not have remained a mighty nation with no cause for further disunion, and able as the war had shown to place in the field more than two million fighting men?

Is it not equally unnecessary to urge, as if it were a valid excuse for our government's refusal to exchange, that between the two nations there would have been frequent if not perpetual hostilities? Why so, any more than between the United States and Canada, where for fifty (it is now a hundred) years, along a boundary line of thirty-eight hundred miles, there had been unbroken peace and no fort nor warship?

Let us not raise the question whether Lincoln made a colossal blunder when he renounced his favorite doctrine so emphatically set forth in his Congressional speech (page 47). The die was cast when Sumter was fired on. The question which confronted him in 1863-64—What to do with the perishing Union prisoners?—was simply one of military necessity.

According to the ethics of war was he not fully justified in sacrificing us rather than imperiling the great cause which he had at heart?

Are we, then, to blame President Davis, or the Confederate Commissioner Robert Ould, or Gen. John H. Winder, Superintendent of Military Prisons, for allowing the Federal prisoners to starve and freeze and die by thousands? Must we not admit the truth of their contention that their soldiers needed the food, clothing, and medical care for want of which their prisoners were suffering? And if the shocking conditions at Andersonville, Salisbury, Danville, and other prisons could easily have been avoided, or even if they were made more distressing by the deliberate inhumanity of those in immediate charge, ought not such facts to have intensified a desire on the part of both governments to effect a speedy exchange?

The southern people were threatened with subjugation, their government with annihilation. In such a critical situation, what measures are allowable?

We endeavor to look at the matter from both standpoints.

This brings up the whole question of the rightfulness of war. If it must be waged, is success the highest duty? If military necessity demands, may any and every law of God and man be disregarded?

While we write these concluding pages, the European conflict is raging, and the voice of the most warlike nation on the globe is heard continually affirming that war is useful and highly honorable, and that any means, however frightful, if necessary to ensure or hasten victory is praise-worthy!

Then both presidents were right!

But is not international war murder on a great scale? It is glorious to die for one's country; but how about killing for our country? killing innocent men, too? for the soldiers on either side honestly believe they are doing their duty in shooting and stabbing as many as possible! "The business of war," said John Wesley, "is the business of devils." So it would seem; but at heart few are enemies, none devils.

It has been a pleasure in this narrative to record instances of a very different spirit. Surely, in proportion to population such were not fewer in the South than in the North. Like Whittier's *Angels of Buena Vista* they rescue us from pessimism. They are prophetic of a better day.

Not wholly lost, O Father, is this evil world of ours!
Upward through the blood and ashes spring afresh the Eden flowers:
From its smoking hell of battle, Love and Pity send their prayer,
And still thy white-winged angels hover dimly in our air!

FOOTNOTES:

[11] I still possess the copy of Davies's *Legendre* which I bought on the 8th of November for twenty Confederate dollars, and of which I memorized three books in prison. As to the *Shakespeare*, see *ante*, p. 85.

[12] I retain with pride the wooden spoon which did me good service when I was *in limbo*. It cost me over two weeks' labor in shaping it with half a knife-blade and pieces of broken glass. For the little block of wood I paid the sentry one "rebel dollar!"

[13] Many years after the war he rendered financial aid to fellow prisoners, his chum, artist Vander Weyde, and General Hayes. Author of several valuable works, he is now head of the publishing house of G. P. Putnam's Sons.

[14] It was a special pleasure after the lapse of fifty years to meet Estabrooks at the Massachusetts Commandery of the Loyal Legion, where, without knowing of his presence, I had just made honorable mention of him in an address on prison life.

[15] In my own case the prison experience was peculiar: it changed the course of my whole subsequent life. I had studied law, been admitted to the bar in two states, and "practiced" with fair success, "though," as a friend was accustomed to remark, "not enough to do much harm!" Many times one of the best men I ever knew, my father, had said to me at parting, "Do all the good you can." Much meditating while in the army and especially while in prison, I finally resolved to pursue an educational career. Of course I felt sadly the loss of years of study that might have better equipped me; but it seemed a duty. I had had some experience which, I thought, proved me not wholly unqualified. While a student in college and while reading law I had partly supported myself by giving instruction to private pupils and in the schools of General Russell and Mayor Skinner. Afterwards, before the war, I had taught Greek in the Worcester (Mass.) Academy; and English literature, Greek, and Latin for more than three years as principal of the Worcester public high school. I knew the vocation would be congenial. So I became principal of a state normal school, of two high schools, of a large academy; house chairman of a (Conn.) legislative committee securing the enactment of three school measures of importance; later, president of a college, professor in a theological seminary and in Cornell University; founder and for three years first president of the earliest and long the largest of the world's general *summer* schools (which now in the United States number nearly 700); lecturer in many Chautauqua assemblies, colleges, vacation schools, and university extension centres; President of the State University of North Dakota; editor, with biographic sketches and copious notes, of many masterpieces as text-books in higher English literature; author of a history of my regiment; also of a treatise on *Voice and Gesture*, of many monographs and magazine articles mostly educational; associate founder and first president of *The Watch and Ward Society*; one of the directors and executive committee of the *American Peace Society*; director of the *Massachusetts Peace Society*; president of *The American Institute of Instruction*; translator, annotator, and essayist of *The Book of Job*; etc.

It may be proper to add that among those indebted in some degree to my instruction or training were several who captured Yale's highest prize for rhetorical excellence (the hundred dollar gold medal of which I was the first recipient): one college president; six college professors; three university presidents; two governors of states; two United States Senators; and many others eminent as clergymen, authors, judges, editors, and business men.

[16] The higher death-rate (if that be conceded) of southern soldiers is easily accounted for. The northern soldiers had been carefully selected by competent surgeons. They were physically perfect, or nearly so. They were in the bloom of early manhood or the strength of middle age—not an old man among them, not a diseased man among them, not a broken-down constitution among them. But multitudes of the southern, enrolled by conscription, were physically unfit. Many were much too old or too young. Said our General Grant, "To fill their ranks, they have robbed the cradle and the grave!"

[17] The exchange is said to have been stopped in 1862-63 by the refusal of the Confederates to give up captured negro soldiers in return for southern captives in the North, the United States properly insisting upon perfect equality in the treatment of black and white. But early in 1864, if not previously, the Confederates yielded the point and were anxious to surrender man for man.

APPENDIX

(From the original record. See p. 88.)

PROCEEDINGS of a Court Martial convened at Danville Mil. Pris. by virtue of the following Order:

DANVILLE MIL. PRISON, Oct. 29, 1864.

General Order

No. 1.

Pursuant to the Regulations adopted by the Union Officers of the 2d Floor Military Prison, Danville, Va., Oct. 26, 1864, a Court Martial is hereby appointed to convene at 10 o'clock A.M. on the 29th inst. or as soon thereafter as may be practicable, for the Trial of Captain [I omit from the record the name of the accused], 104th N. Y. Vols., and such other officers as may be brought before it.

Detail for the Court.

Lt. Col. W. A. LEACH,
90th P. V.
Lt. Col. THEO. GREGG,
45th P. V.
Major J. W. BYRON,
88th N. Y. V.
Capt. G. M. DICKERMAN,
26th Mass. V.

[Here follow the names of Captains Bryant, Black, Clapp, Burkart, Weiss (?), Reilly (?), Moody, and the name of the Judge Advocate, Lt. and Adjt. James A. Clark, 17th Pa. Cav.]

By order of the Officers of the 2d Floor,
JAMES CARLE,
Col. 190th Pa. Vols., Senior Officer.

DANVILLE MIL. PRISON, VA., 10 o'clock A.M., 31st, Oct. 1864.

The Court met pursuant to the foregoing order. Present all the members. The Court then proceeded to the trial of Capt. [we again omit the name of the accused], 104th N. Y. Vols.

The Judge Advocate stated that he had acquainted the accused of the order convening the Court, to which he replied in the words following, to wit: "What is that to do with me? I recognize no authority in this prison to convene a court martial," or words to that effect.

The accused having refused to appear, the members of the Court were duly sworn by the Judge Advocate, and the Judge Advocate was duly sworn by the President of the Court. The accused, Capt. [again we omit the name], 104th N. Y. Vols., was arraigned on the following charges and specifications:

Charge—Conduct unbecoming an officer and a gentleman.

Specification—In this: That Capt. [we again omit], 104th N. Y. Vols., without provocation, did say in the hearing of several officers to Lieut. Col. Homer B. Sprague, 13th C. V., speaking in coarse and ungentlemanly manner the words following, to wit: [here we omit the language uttered as being too vile and filthy to print]; that he did several times repeat the same in a coarse and angry tone, and used other vulgar and indecent expressions in an insulting tone and manner. This at Danville Mil. Prison, Va., in the lower room thereof on the 29th day of October, 1864.

The accused refusing to appear, the Judge Advocate was directed by the President to enter the plea of Not Guilty.

To the Specification, Not Guilty.
To the Charge, Not Guilty.

Lieut. G. C. Wilson, 2d P. Artillery, and Lieut. Wm. Shuler, 107th P. Vols., witnesses for the prosecution, stated that they had cognizance of the facts set forth in the Specification.

The proceedings of the Court having been reviewed by the Judge Advocate, he submitted the case without argument. The Court was then cleared for deliberation, and having maturely considered the evidence adduced find the accused

On the Specification, Guilty; with the exception of the words "and used other vulgar and indecent expressions."

Of the Charge, Guilty. And do therefore sentence him to be reprimanded by the Senior Officer.

The Court is thus lenient owing to this being the first case of the kind brought before it.

WM. A. LEACH, Lt. Col. 90th Regt. Pa. Vols., Pres.;
JAS. A. CLARK, Adjt. 17th Pa. Cavalry, Judge Advocate.

The Proceedings and Findings in the foregoing case are hereby respectfully submitted to Brig.-Gen. Hayes for his consideration.

JAMES CARLE, Col. 191st Pa. Vols., Senior Officer, 2d Floor.

CONFED. MIL. PRISON, DANVILLE, VA., Nov. 1, 1864.

The Proceedings and Findings of the Court Martial of which Lt. Col. W. A. Leach, 90th Pa. Vols., was President, having been submitted to Brig.-Gen. Hayes, the Senior Officer present, are approved. The extreme leniency of the Court must be apparent to all, and can only be excused by the novelty of the case brought before it. Language fails to convey censure adequate to the gross vulgarity and ungentlemanly conduct of the accused. Captain [we omit the name] seems to forget or misconceive his responsibility in his present circumstances. An officer being a prisoner of war is not relieved from his responsibility to his government nor from his liability to the regulations of the service as far as may be applied to his dishonor by ungentlemanly and unofficer-like conduct; and many other offenses committed by an officer when a prisoner of war are as punishable as if that officer were serving with his command. And it is well the officers in the prison have organized a Court for the summary punishment of those of their number, who, forgetful of their position and their honor, would bring shame upon themselves and their associates.

It is to be hoped that Capt. [name we omit]'s conduct in the future will be such as will cause to be forgotten his mistakes of the past.

JOSEPH HAYES, Brig. Gen. U. S. Vols.

www.ingramcontent.com/pod-product-compliance
Lightning Source LLC
Chambersburg PA
CBHW080910190726
48294CB00008B/2033
* 9 7 8 1 8 3 5 5 2 5 0 1 2 *